PRODUCT LIABILITY

The Law and its Implications for Risk Management

PRODUCT LIABILITY

The Law and its Implications for Risk Management

Christopher J. Wright, BA, LLM, Cert Ed
Senior Lecturer in Commercial Law, Staffordshire Polytechnic

BLACKSTONE
PRESS LIMITED

First published in Great Britain 1989 by Blackstone Press Limited,
9–15 Aldine Street, London W12 8AW. Telephone 01-740 1173

© Christopher J. Wright, 1989

ISBN: 1 85431 036 4

British Library Cataloguing in Publication Data
A CIP catalogue record for this book is available from the British Library

Typeset by Style Photosetting Ltd, Mayfield, East Sussex
Printed by Billing & Sons Ltd, Worcester

Contents

5   Criminal Liability   89

The general safety requirement — Safety regulations — Due diligence defence — Further powers and enforcement — Criminal liability for non-consumer goods — Other products not covered by the general safety requirement or by safety regulations issued under the Consumer Protection Act 1987 — Who is liable for an offence: the individual or the organisation he works for? — Avoiding criminal liability — Summary — Notes

PART 2   MANAGING THE PRODUCT LIABILITY RISK   111

6   Defects   113

Manufacturing defect — Design defect — Warning or instruction defect — Summary — Notes

7   Incriminating Evidence   143

Discovery — Interrogatories — Depositions — Progress of the case to trial — What are they looking for? The 'smoking gun', the 'unexploded bomb' and the 'open loop' — Avoiding incriminating evidence in written communications and documents — Summary — Notes

8   General Management Strategy   169

Commitment to product safety — Training and motivating staff — Forming a product safety committee — Product safety coordinator — Risk strategy — Planning for the unthinkable — Recall — Summary — Notes

9   Responsibilities of Particular Departments and Functions   185

Research and development, product engineering, design — Purchasing — Manufacturing, assembly, installation, repair — Quality and inspection — Sales and marketing — Service and after-sales support — Finance — Legal — Personnel and training — Summary

Appendix 1   BS 5750: Summary of Main Factors Considered in Meeting the Standard   203

Index   211

Preface

Recent developments in product liability law are of enormous significance for manufacturers, distributors and consumers. Following implementation of an EEC Directive in Britain, via the Consumer Protection Act 1987, a victim of a defective product no longer need establish negligence by the producer to succeed in a claim for compensation. Britain and the rest of the EEC are adopting a 'no-fault' or 'strict liability' concept, similar to that operating in the United States. Proposed changes to the system of legal representation in Britain, the possibility of contingency fee lawyers ('no win no fee') and pressure for higher awards are further examples of the move towards American-style rights for victims. New criminal offences and enforcement powers make prosecution of suppliers of unsafe products more likely.

This is great news for victims. It could prove very expensive for producers and suppliers, who will be looking for ways to minimise their legal exposure.

This book sets out the current law on product liability in the UK and its implications for producers and suppliers. It provides practical advice on methods of reducing the risk of marketing a defective product, of defending claims when they arise, and of effective risk management. It points out the pitfalls for individuals, departments and organisations. A major theme is that legal exposure can be created unnecessarily through lack of awareness and failure to implement simple risk management techniques.

The book should provide an invaluable guide to managers, legal practitioners and students of law and business management.

Acknowledgements

I would like to express my gratitude to all those who helped and encouraged me to complete this book. In particular Robert Grant, Company Solicitor, and Roger Schofield, Senior Training Officer, at Jaguar Cars Ltd for helping organise the many sessions with designers, engineers and other Jaguar personnel, both in Britain and America, to discuss the practical issues of Product Safety.

Thanks to Alistair MacQueen and Heather Saward of Blackstone Press Ltd for applying appropriate pressure and for the remarkably fast transition from draft manuscript to completed text: to Derek French for his editorial skills; to colleagues at Staffordshire Polytechnic for their forbearance and to Sue Wright for her constant support and advice.

Any defects in the final product are entirely my own responsibility.

Table of Cases

Table of Statutes

PART I
THE LAW AND ITS IMPLICATIONS

1

The Legal Background

You will already be aware that there are numerous laws, regulations, standards and codes of practice which try to ensure that products and services meet appropriate levels of quality and safety, also that the methods of trading, the terms imposed and any attempts to exclude or limit liability are fair and reasonable.

Failure to meet these requirements can result in both *civil and criminal liabilities* (a civil action is undertaken to provide compensation or other forms of redress to the purchaser or victim; a criminal prosecution can result in fines and/or imprisonment or other penalties imposed by the authorities).

Major new legislation in the Consumer Protection Act 1987 has changed the basis on which a victim can sue a producer, introduced new criminal offences and extended the powers of the safety enforcement authorities.

'Product liability' is generally taken as referring to the civil liability of a manufacturer or distributor for damage or injury caused by a defect in the product. Under English law a victim of a defective product has two legal routes under which to sue for compensation:

(a) If he were the buyer of the product (or had entered into any other sort of contract, such as hire-purchase or lease) then he could base his claim on *breach of contract*. The law of contract provides him with excellent rights to pursue his claim, laid down in statutes such as the Sale of Goods Act 1979. The key factor is that there is no need to prove fault by the seller: the mere fact that the product does not conform to the contractual expectation is enough. So even if the seller was in no way to blame, e.g.,

a shopkeeper sells a product in a sealed container which he could not be
expected to check before resale, that seller would still be liable. This
concept is known as 'strict liability'.

The problem with a contractual claim is that only the parties to that contract can
sue and be sued: a concept known as 'privity of contract'. The buyer (hirer etc.)
sues the immediate seller (lessor etc.), typically a shop or dealer rather than the
actual manufacturer of the product. Unless the manufacturer sold directly to the
consumer or provided a guarantee, then he has no contractual relationship with
that consumer. So the shop pays the compensation. It could then try to recover
on its contract with its supplier, and so on back to the manufacturer of the
product or of the component part responsible for the defect. All well and good
if the shop is able to pay and to sue those before it in the distribution chain but if
it cannot then no one receives compensation.

(b)   For a victim who was not party to a contract (e.g., a bystander, a user
       other than the buyer, a recipient of a gift), there is no contractual
       remedy. His route is under the *law of tort* (a tort is a civil wrong other
       than a breach of contract). A number of different torts might apply, but
       until the 1987 Act by far the most important was *negligence*. This means
       breach of a duty to take reasonable care, resulting in damage or injury. The
       victim can sue anyone he thinks responsible, e.g., the manufacturer of
       the finished product, the manufacturer of a component part, the shop
       which failed to check or the owner who failed to maintain the product in
       good order. Unlike contract, his claim is not limited to the immediate
       supplier.

The big problem with negligence is in proving there was a lack of *reasonable
care:* success depends on proof of fault. Generally the burden of proof is on the
plaintiff (victim), who must find sufficient evidence to prove, on a balance of
probabilities, that the defendant failed to take reasonable care. That is not
always easy. The defendant can argue that he did his best: the defect slipped
through despite excellent quality control; it was impractical to carry out
additional inspection; the risk was unforeseeable etc. The time and cost
involved in pursuing a negligence claim may cause the plaintiff to drop his case
or accept a pretrial settlement for less than he might otherwise obtain. As a
result many victims of defective products have been denied compensation.

The new system under the Consumer Protection Act 1987 renders a 'producer'
of a defective product *strictly liable* for personal injury or damage to personal
property, i.e., without proof of negligence or the need for a contractual
relationship. We have changed from a *fault-based* to a *no-fault* concept of liability

in respect of defective products causing damage or injury to any person, though there are limitations and exceptions where the Act will not apply. The move follows pressure from consumers, the Law Commission and the European Commission to create better rights for victims.

This is great news for consumers. It could be very expensive for manufacturers and distributors.

In the United States strict liability for defective products has operated for a number of years (with variations between the individual States). Throughout this book there are references to American cases which, while not binding on English courts, provide a useful guide to how the concept applies in practice.

Does this mean a move towards American-style litigation and size of awards? Is it an inevitable step towards the 'product liability crisis' experienced in that country, where manufacturers have been bankrupted by enormous awards to victims, insurance premiums have sky-rocketed and products have been pulled off the market? There are certainly likely to be more successful cases brought by victims, and costs and insurance premiums for producers will reflect this, but not to the same extent as in the USA. The American legal environment, rather than the principle of strict liability itself, is responsible for that crisis, which has now been alleviated by reforms in the law.

Contributory factors in the American environment include:

(a)   The general willingness of Americans to take legal action, with a system which encourages rather than deters litigation.

(b)   The high costs of medical care and rehabilitation, reflected in the size of awards. Britain's National Health Service and social security system lessen such costs for the individual victim.

(c)   Jury trial, where the jury not only decides whether the producer is liable, but also the size of the award. Juries tend to be sympathetic and generous, especially at the sight of a poor injured victim in a court room up against some mighty corporation. In Britain the practice is not to use a jury in product liability actions.

(d)   Punitive damages, which may be awarded on top of the compensation for injury where the jury considers the producer has acted negligently, recklessly or with wanton disregard for safety. Sometimes this results in multi-million-dollar awards.[1] The aim is to punish the producer, but the award goes to the victim. In Britain punitive (or exemplary) damages are rarely awarded, and their justification has been seriously questioned by the courts.

(e)   The contingency fee system (no win no fee) operated by most American trial lawyers. Usually the fee is based on a percentage of the award. With some of the huge awards that have been made, the lawyers can make a fortune.[2] This has led to so called 'ambulance-chasing', making lawyers extremely keen to win a case once they have agreed to take it on rather than drop it, and willing to spend a great deal of money in gathering evidence, getting experts' reports, reconstructing accidents etc.[3] This expense is reflected in the size of the eventual award. The system means that victims are not deterred from bringing an action by lack of means to pay legal fees.[4]

(f)   Legal costs: generally each side bears its own costs, whereas in Britain the loser normally pays the other side's costs. Another incentive for the victim of poorer means to risk pursuing an action. Also it does not deter doubtful claims, which would not be pursued in Britain, though this is usually prevented by contingency-fee lawyers' unwillingness to take on a baseless case. The producer or distributor may offer a pre-trial settlement to avoid these costs, even when he has a good chance of successfully defending.

There are a number of other factors which place producers in a more vulnerable position than in Britain, even with the introduction of strict liability. The proposed reforms[5] of the English system of legal representation may make it easier and cheaper for victims to pursue claims, but should not lead to the American excesses. For example, a contingency fee system would probably only allow the standard fee to be paid on winning, not a percentage of the award. While there are lessons to be learned from the American experience, the impact will not be so devastating.[6]

AIM OF THIS BOOK

Unlike a standard legal text, this book is not simply concerned with the detail of the law but with its practical implications, in particular the steps that can be taken to reduce the potential legal exposure. Often such exposure may be created unnecessarily through a lack of awareness by staff of the possible legal implications of their actions, comments, wording of reports, handling of complaints etc.

Chapters 2 to 5 examine the legal provisions and their implications, with guidance on the tactics that can be used by a producer or distributor to minimise the possibility of incurring liability. While these chapters refer to English law, similar principles apply in other countries whose legal system is based on the common law, such as the USA, Canada, Australia and many former colonial territories. Within the European Community the move towards harmonisation through implementation of EEC Directives and Regulations means that victims of defective products now have broadly similar rights against producers, though some significant differences remain (as discussed at the end of chapter 3). It will be emphasised that while the law provides excellent rights for victims, there are provisos and defences available to producers.

Chapters 6 to 9 discuss the strategies that can be adopted to avoid marketing a defective product in the first place and to handle product liability claims if they do arise. Managing the product liability risk is a matter of being aware of the legal implications throughout the processes of design, manufacture and marketing of a product and then taking effective steps to eliminate or minimise the risks. This does not just mean applying standards, procedures and resources to ensure the product meets high levels of quality and safety: *it also means making staff at all levels and in all functions aware of the possible implications of their words and actions.* A producer can have the best design and manufacturing techniques available, yet a lack of awareness by staff can cause unnecessary legal exposure.

A typical example is the service representative who greets the complaining customer with: 'It's a common fault with these machines. They're all like it. Poor design'. How does he know that it is a poor design? He is not a design engineer. It may be that the part is designed to break in certain circumstances in a safe failure mode, rather than surviving and causing some other safety-critical part to break. Car bodies are designed to absorb crashes by crumbling progressively, yet on seeing an accident-damaged car many repairers will agree with the customer that the body panels are damaged too easily, and that: 'They don't make them as strong as they used to'. Such comments give the customer (or his lawyer) ammunition to use against the producer. It is not too difficult in the above examples to discredit the comments, but they do not help the producer's defence.

Another example is the exaggeration or dramatisation of a problem on a report to try to make someone take notice. The originator feels that unless he makes it sound very serious nothing will be done; that the person to whom he is sending the report has a pile of other problems, and the only way to get this one to the top of the pile is to add comments such as: 'Unless urgent action is taken, someone could be badly injured'. Any injury might in fact be extremely remote and minor, so the responsible producer would be correct in giving a lower priority to solving that problem while attending to the really serious ones. If an accident later occurs that report could fall into the hands of a lawyer acting for a victim and would be interpreted as an admission that a serious problem existed, leading to allegations of negligence or reckless disregard for safety.

The theme throughout this book is that a responsible producer can take effective steps to manage the product liability risk. Not by devious tactics, denying problems exist, refusing to write down anything to do with safety or shredding potentially incriminating documents, but by adopting sensible policies and by educating his staff on the importance of product safety.

NOTES

1   Many States have now put ceilings on punitive damages and/or restricted the circumstances in which they can be awarded because of the effect in bankrupting producers, making certain products unobtainable and increasing prices.

2   These percentages vary, depending on the nature of the case, typically around 25–30%. Many States have now introduced limits on fees, the general pattern being a decreasing percentage as the award increases.

3   The American Trial Lawyers' Association maintains a computer-based file of information on particular products, with details of claims brought against them, settlements made etc. making it easier for a lawyer to build up a picture of the history of the product, its manufacturer and distributors as evidence of a pattern of failure.

4   The English system of legal aid is not an effective alternative.

5   In three government Green Papers issued on 25 January 1989: *The Work and Organisation of the Legal Profession* (Cm 570), *Contingency Fees* (Cm 571) and *Conveyancing by Authorised Practitioners* (Cm 572).

6   American laws obviously affect UK manufacturers exporting to the United States, who may be brought directly into American proceedings through the Hague Convention procedure. Less obvious is the fact that a UK component manufacturer who supplies a UK end-product manufacturer may also become involved in US litigation if the end-product is exported there.

2

Civil Liability under The Law of Contract

English Law has developed two distinct forms of civil liability:

(a) *Breach of contract* — a failure to fulfil an agreement.

(b) *Tort* — a civil wrong (as opposed to a crime) such as negligence, nuisance or breach of other legal duties.

CONTRACT

Contract is the basis of commercial dealings. The law recognises that once an agreement has been made (whether verbal or written), then the parties are bound by it and can turn to the courts for a remedy if it is broken.

To be a legally enforceable contract the agreement has to satisfy certain criteria. There must be: an offer and an acceptance in terms sufficiently clear to amount to a firm agreement; some element of 'consideration' i.e., money, goods, labour or other item of economic value exchanged between the parties (so pure gifts are not contractual unless the special form of contract known as a 'contract under seal' is used); the parties must have 'capacity' to contract (so contracts with minors, drunkards etc. cannot always be enforced); and there must be an intention to create a legal relationship (so many purely social or domestic arrangements do not incur legal liabilities if broken).[1]

The sale or hire of goods or services will therefore form a contract.

The ensuing discussion will refer to 'sales of goods' with a 'seller' and a 'buyer', though similar rules apply to credit, hire-purchase, lease and other forms of supply.

Most types of contract do not have to be put in writing. An agreement to sell goods, however expensive, is a perfectly valid contract if made verbally or indeed by gestures. The vast majority of everyday consumer contracts are not written: imagine the delays if everyone buying an article of food or household commodity insisted on a written agreement detailing the terms of the purchase!

The problem with not having something in writing, of course, is that it makes it difficult to prove afterwards just what was agreed if a dispute arises. For that reason many businesses use purchasing and sales documents, containing both standard terms (usually printed on the reverse) and the details of the individual contract (typed or handwritten on the front). Even with these an alteration can be made verbally, which will actually take precedence over the written term. For example, a purchase order may state that the goods are to meet a certain specification: the supplier then telephones to say he has none of those in stock, so would an alternative be acceptable? A verbal agreement to that request will supersede the original written specification, even though no written confirmation is made of it. Again the problem of proof arises.

How can such proof be found? Ultimately it may depend solely on people's memories, and if these conflict a court might have to conclude that no firm agreement was ever reached. However, there may be other evidence: witnesses to the conversation; a pattern of dealing over a period between the parties; the actions of the parties which indicate they were acting consistently with a particular agreement.

A common situation is where a customer returns to the supplier and complains: 'You told me the goods would be . . .'

To which the supplier replies: 'No, I didn't. What I said was . . .'

A useful weapon for the supplier in such a situation is to follow a procedure of always explaining certain things to customers at the time of sale: e.g., sales representatives could be trained to show *all* customers the manufacturer's brochure, explain how the thing works, give them instruction leaflets, check they understand etc. The supplier can then claim: 'We have a procedure whereby we always tell customers . . .'

Other customers could support this claim.

While such evidence would only be circumstantial in a court of law, it might well be enough to persuade the customer to drop his complaint.

EXPRESS AND IMPLIED TERMS

In a contract for a sale or supply of goods there will be both *expressly agreed* terms and additional terms *implied by law.*

The implied terms are necessary because generally the parties do not discuss certain aspects of the contract when they make the agreement, e.g., when buying an item of food one will expressly agree with the sales assistant the type and quantity required and the price. That is all. In a supermarket this will be done simply by placing goods on the checkout conveyor and the cashier entering the price. With larger items perhaps a method of packaging and delivery is also arranged.

One does not normally say: 'Can we agree what my rights will be if there is a dead insect inside the food?'

Here the law *implies* certain rights and duties into the contract. These implied terms state (in summary and subject to certain provisos discussed later) that the goods must:

(a)   meet the description applied to them;

(b)   be of merchantable quality;

(c)   be reasonably fit for the particular purpose for which they are supplied;

(d)   correspond with the sample in quality, if bought on the basis of a sample.

It should be noted that these terms cover all aspects of the goods, not just their safety.

So the buyer will have a remedy when he swallows the insect.

These implied terms add to, or sometimes replace, the expressly agreed terms. So even if there is an express term, the buyer may have additional rights: for example, the food wrapper might have on it: 'If you are not satisfied with this product please return it and we will be pleased to send you a replacement', or an offer of reimbursement. This may not be a lot of use when the buyer is suffering from shock and food poisoning! Such consequential damage can (at least in a consumer sale, see below) be claimed under the contract, despite the limits which the wrapper statement purports to impose.

In business-to-business transactions detailed terms will usually be set out in writing, and in consumer purchases of larger items, such as cars or electrical appliances, one does perhaps discuss what is to happen when the thing goes wrong. Usually some form of 'guarantee' or 'warranty' is given with the product, offering to repair or replace defective parts within a certain period.

EFFECT OF A GUARANTEE

With new goods a guarantee is normally given by the manufacturer, who in the typical consumer sale does not deal directly with the ultimate purchaser. The chain of supply will involve one or more distributors (importer, wholesaler, dealer, shop etc.) each selling on to the next until the product reaches the consumer. If the consumer has a complaint, then his prime target is the immediate seller from whom he bought the goods, i.e., with whom he made the contract.

It is into that contract that the law implies the terms, irrespective of any manufacturer's guarantee.

So a guarantee is an *addition* to the buyer's rights under the contract with the *seller* (e.g., shop). These rights cannot be taken away from a private consumer, and it is a legal requirement that on any statement offering remedies to consumers there must also be a statement to the effect that 'This does not affect your statutory rights'.[2]

Armed with a guarantee the buyer therefore has two contractual routes for seeking redress: under the main contract with the seller, *and* under the terms of the guarantee with the manufacturer. That guarantee may be regarded legally as a 'collateral contract',[3] enforceable by the parties (even though there is no direct contract between them), but always in addition to the main contract.

However, there is no legal obligation to give a guarantee in the first place, and it can contain limitations.[4] It may be conditional on the customer filling out and returning a card. It may be granted only to the original purchaser, and be not transferable to subsequent owners. A charge may be made for 'extended' guarantees. Most guarantees limit the remedy to repair or replacement within a time-limit, and sometimes only for certain parts of the product.

So when the door of the washing machine breaks, the customer might get a new door fitted free of charge, but nothing *under the guarantee* for the flooded kitchen. If the brakes on the car fail within 12 months of purchase, he may get new brake parts, but nothing for the injury in the ensuing crash.

Those consequential damages may be claimable under the main contract of sale with the immediate seller, i.e., from the shop that sold the washing machine or the dealer who supplied the car. If that seller pays out compensation, he in turn has a contract back to his supplier under which he can try to claim that loss as arising from a breach of that contract, and so on back through the links in the distribution chain. The manufacturer will probably end up paying, but not through a direct contractual claim from the customer.

A customer who knows his rights should not therefore be put off by the limitations of any guarantee. He can always use his rights under the contract with the shop or dealer.

The customer can sue the manufacturer directly under *other* legal routes (e.g., negligence or breach of the Consumer Protection Act 1987 — see chapters 3 and 4). But why should he bother when he has adequate rights against the seller?

In practice because it is easier. The consumer will normally be quite happy with the repair or replacement offered under the guarantee, rather than claiming money from a resisting seller. The washing-machine manufacturer may, as a goodwill gesture, pay for the damage to the kitchen. Perhaps the seller has meanwhile gone out of business and so cannot pay.

Despite the laws on consumer rights and their media coverage, there are still many consumers *and* retailers who seem oblivious to the legal position. Complaining customers are frequently met with the response from the retailer: 'Nothing to do with us. Take it up with the manufacturer under the guarantee.'

The retailer is wrong, but without an argument and the possible threat of legal action he is unlikely to pay up.

Another advantage of a guarantee to the customer is that it may cover minor defects which would not otherwise amount to a breach of contract (e.g., six-year anti-corrosion on a car).

From the manufacturer's point of view the guarantee shows he is prepared to stand by his goods, which may enhance his reputation and perhaps his sales as a result. He should remember that no matter how good the guarantee might be, it must indicate that the consumer's statutory rights are not affected. Failure to do so is a criminal offence.[5] Many businesses, through ignorance or indifference, are continuing to use notices, sales documents and packaging containing illegal notices. These include companies generally regarded as highly reputable, who would never knowingly commit an offence.

TERMS AND REPRESENTATIONS

Contracts for the sale or supply of goods are regulated under English law by various statutes. In relation to contractual liability for quality and safety, the Sale of Goods Act 1979, the Supply of Goods (Implied Terms) Act 1973 and the Supply of Goods and Services Act 1982 contain the all-important implied terms. For convenience, only the Sale of Goods Act 1979 will be considered, referring to 'seller' and 'buyer'. The other Acts deal with forms of supply other than sale, but the relevant terms are almost identically worded.[6] The Unfair Contract Terms Act 1977 regulates the use of exemption clauses purporting to limit or exclude liability for breach of these terms.

The combination of expressly agreed and implied terms creates the contractual obligations of the supplier. Liability can also arise for *misrepresentation*. A representation is a statement made *before* the contract is agreed which induces the other party to enter into it, e.g., in sales brochures and pre-contract negotiations. The Misrepresentation Act 1967 provides remedies if such statements are untrue, even if made innocently.[7]

APPLICATION OF THE IMPLIED TERMS IN A CONTRACT OF SALE

The implied terms mentioned above appear in the Sale of Goods Act 1979, ss. 13 to 15. These give considerable rights to buyers, but there are various tactics available to a seller to make use of the provisos and exceptions within those sections. Equally the buyer can adopt converse tactics to his benefit.

Description

Sale of Good Act 1979, s. 13(1):

Where there is a contract for the sale of goods by description, there is an implied condition that the goods will correspond with the description

It is only fair that if the buyer gets something different to that described when he made the contract he should have a remedy. Most misdescriptions are simple mistakes: the wrong goods are delivered, the box is incorrectly labelled etc.

Most do not cause any physical damage: the buyer is merely inconvenienced and may suffer financial loss through delay in getting the correct goods.

However, there are circumstances where physical damage could result: suppose an electric motor were incorrectly described as having an automatic cut-out, or a car as having 'run-flat' tyres, and injury occurred through the user assuming he was protected.

Cases suggest that a small deviation between what is described and what is delivered can amount to a breach of the condition. In one case[8] the contract involved lengths of wood for making barrels. The specification for the thickness was 1/2 inch. The buyer found that only a small proportion were precisely 1/2 inch, the majority varying up to 9/16 inch. While this variation did not make the wood unsuitable for the intended purpose, the buyer chose to reject. The court held he was entitled to do so.

In other cases the courts have taken a more flexible approach,[9] but the message for a seller is clear: if you cannot be accurate, give a margin of tolerance.

The seller's tactics, therefore:

● Keep descriptions to a minimum.

● Ensure descriptions are totally accurate. If unsure, check, don't guess.

● Put tolerances on specifications (e.g., 'approx. 1/2 inch', 'nominal', 'sizes may vary').

● Inform the buyer that goods may be different at the time of delivery to the description in the brochure etc., i.e., that he should not rely on that description.

A common statement is: 'Seller reserves the right to alter the specification without notice'. Just how effective such a notice might be if challenged is not clear from case law. Presumably it allows the seller to make minor changes, but not to supply something fundamentally different.[10]

Buyer's tactics:

● Ask for detailed specifications.

● Challenge vague statements.

● Ask questions, preferably in writing, and demand written answers.

● Insist the contract is based on the specification currently offered, not subject to later variation (unless this can only be favourable).

Merchantable quality

Sale of Goods Act 1979, s. 14(2):

Where the seller sells goods in the course of a business, there is an implied condition that the goods supplied under the contract are of merchantable quality, except that there is no such condition —

(a)   as regards defects specifically drawn to the buyer's attention before the contract is made; or

(b)   if the buyer examines the goods before the contract is made, as regards defects which that examination ought to reveal.

This implied condition, together with fitness for purpose under s. 14(3), applies only when the supply is *in the course of a business*, so private sellers are not covered. If unmerchantable or unfit goods are bought from a private seller the buyer's only contractual remedy is for misdescription or breach of an *express* promise by the seller as to quality or fitness. The old maxim, *caveat emptor* (let the buyer beware), still applies to private sales.

Any sale in the course of a business is included, even of goods not normally sold. A grocer is therefore liable both for the quality of the food he sells as his regular business, and for any one-off sales such as the surplus delivery van, office typewriter etc. 'Business' includes not only manufacturing and trade, but also professions (e.g., accountants), government departments, local and public authorities. It need not be a profit-making business.[11]

The provision applies to 'goods supplied', which includes any packaging, free gifts or other accessories. If the box in which the goods are packed collapses, then the seller is liable for the damage caused, even though the box may be free and remain the seller's property.[12]

It also applies to instructions and warnings supplied with the goods.[13] The adequacy of warnings is discussed in chapter 6.

What is meant by 'merchantable quality'? Section 14(6) offers a short definition:

> Goods of any kind are of merchantable quality . . . if they are as fit for the
> purpose or purposes for which goods of that kind are commonly bought as it
> is reasonable to expect having regard to any description applied to them, the
> price (if relevant) and all the other relevant circumstances.

This does not really give a lot of help. If the goods have minor faults, or one out
of a hundred delivered is defective, does this make them unmerchantable? What
if they are suitable for most purposes but not every possible purpose for which
they might be bought? Suppose the defect does not become apparent until
some time later: do the goods have to remain merchantable for a particular time?

Numerous cases have been brought before the courts to interpret and apply the
term to individual situations. Academic writers, the Law Commission[14] and
other commentators have added their opinions and recommendations for an
improved definition.[15] It is not intended here to analyse all these in detail[16] but
to draw certain general conclusions relevant to the seller seeking to minimise
his potential liability:

(a) *The goods do not have to be fit for every purpose for which they might
conceivably be used, only for common purposes.*

If the buyer has a special purpose in mind, he should point this out and rely on s.
14(3) for a remedy (see pages 21–22).

A seller can take positive steps to limit the purpose by statements on the goods
themselves, on instruction manuals, during pre-contract negotiations etc. For
example:

● 'Suitable for the following applications . . .'

● 'Use only indoors'.

● 'Not recommended for . . .'

This is particularly necessary if the product has limitations, dangers or
peculiarities not present on comparable products.

(b) *The goods do not necessarily have to be perfect.*

The standard is what it is reasonable to expect in the circumstances. A new
washing machine which is dented would not be merchantable, even though it
works perfectly, because the buyer does not reasonably expect such a fault; but

if it were sold as 'shop soiled' at a reduced price, or second-hand, then the dent is a reasonable expectation. A clutch defect in a new car would render it unmerchantable; in a second-hand car possibly not,[17] depending on the price and circumstances. A second-hand car described as 'hardly run in' is unmerchantable when the engine seizes up 2,300 miles later,[18] but if described as 'suitable for spares' need not even go. Price is a vital factor, especially with goods of varying quality such as fabrics: the higher the price, the better the standard to be expected.[19]

However, cheapness will not excuse a sale of *unsafe* goods[20] unless the danger has been made apparent.

New goods sold without any indication of faults would normally be expected to be free of any defects, except perhaps very trivial ones.[21] The fact that consumers have got used to putting up with poor quality of certain types of goods does not make them merchantable[22]: the test generally applied is whether the buyer would have bought those goods, at that price, had he known of the defects at the time.[23]

Regarding defects which render the goods unsafe, the cases suggest that even the smallest defect amounts to a breach of condition. Such cases are generally argued on the 'fitness for purpose' provision of s.14(3), rather than merchantability. A distinction can be drawn, however, between a product which *lacks* a safety feature and one which is *intrinsically* defective. A new car which is not fitted with an anti-lock braking system (ABS) is not unmerchantable or unfit, because a buyer does not reasonably expect all cars to have ABS as standard, even though that system may arguably make a car safer. He has the choice: pay more for ABS with its possible advantages, or go for a lower-range model with conventional brakes. It is where those conventional brakes fail to work as expected that the breach occurs.

(c)   *The seller can avoid liability by pointing out defects.*

This proviso is relevant for substandard, second-hand, reconditioned or superseded products. By *specifically* drawing the buyer's attention to the defect, the seller cannot later be liable for *that particular* defect.

Pointing out defects may, of course, so discourage a potential buyer that he does not make a contract. The skilful seller will tactfully draw attention to the defect while extolling the other virtues of the product, particularly any price reduction offered!

Notices such as 'shop-soiled', 'seconds', 'slightly imperfect' have the effect of setting the standard to be expected, but may not always be deemed sufficiently specific to draw attention to defects beyond the normal minor blemishes.

To be sure of benefiting from this proviso, the seller should therefore fully explain the nature of the defect, together with the likely consequences if these are not obvious.

(d)   *The seller will not be liable if the buyer examined the goods and ought to have noticed the defect.*

A buyer is not obliged to examine the goods, and it may be to his advantage not to do so. If he does, then the seller will not be liable for a defect which *that* examination ought to have revealed. So, if the buyer makes a visual examination which would not reveal defects only discoverable under a microscope, then he can claim for such defects.

The seller, particularly when he knows or suspects the goods to be imperfect, should allow the buyer ample opportunity to examine, even to the extent of taking away a sample and testing it to destruction. By adopting such an open policy, the chances of a complaint by the buyer are reduced.

In summary, to benefit from the provisions of s. 14(2) the seller can adopt the following tactics:

- Explain to the buyer what he should expect of the goods at that price, age etc.

- Do not raise the buyer's expectations by exaggerated claims.

- Specifically point out any defects and limitations which are not apparent when the buyer examines the goods.

- Allow the buyer ample opportunity to examine, so he cannot later complain about defects he should have spotted.

Buyer's tactics:

- State what standard you expect as normal.

- Keep a record of any claims made by the seller as to the standard.

- Be aware of the standard achieved by other suppliers of similar products at that time, so that later it can be shown that the normal expectation has not been achieved.

- If offered the opportunity to examine the goods, either do so thoroughly or make it clear that they have not been properly examined.

- Be wary of signing a delivery note stating that the goods are accepted in merchantable condition.

Fitness for purpose

Sale of Goods Act 1979, s. 14(3):

> Where the seller sells goods in the course of a business and the buyer, expressly or by implication, makes known . . . to the seller . . . any particular purpose for which the goods are being bought, there is an implied condition that the goods supplied under the contract are reasonably fit for that purpose, whether or not that is a purpose for which such goods are commonly supplied, except where the circumstances show that the buyer does not rely, or that it is unreasonable for him to rely, on the skill or judgment of the seller.

Like merchantable quality, this implied term only applies to a sale in the course of a business, so private sellers are not affected.

It goes further than s. 14(2) by stating that goods must be not only fit for their common purposes, but also fit for the particular purpose for which the buyer intends to use them. This could be an abnormal purpose.

There are three provisos, behind which the seller can gain some shelter:

(a)   The purpose must be made known.

(b)   The buyer must rely on the seller's skill to supply suitable goods.

(c)   It must be reasonable for the buyer to rely on the seller's skill.

The buyer can only succeed in a claim by satisfying all three provisos.

Where the purpose is obvious, such as food for eating, then there is no need to state that purpose expressly — it is made known by implication. Here s. 14(2) and (3) overlap: if the food is contaminated it is neither merchantable nor fit for eating. If the food is in perfect condition but the buyer is a diabetic, or intends to cook the food in some unusual way, or give it to his highly sensitive pet monkey,[24] then he cannot complain that it is not suitable for that purpose *unless* he satisfies the provisos of s. 14(3). Similarly if the buyer wants a higher standard than would normally be expected.

The purpose may already be known to the seller without the buyer having to communicate it expressly, e.g., where a component supplier knows that the buyer makes a particular finished product or uses a particular process, or a spare-parts supplier knows where the part is likely to be fitted.

The seller can imply fitness by his own actions, so must be careful with his advertising, promotional material, displays, demonstrations and comments about the capabilities of the goods. Sales representatives are prone to extolling the virtues of a product, making out that it can perform all sorts of things, indeed sometimes saying anything that will clinch a sale. A particular danger is when the correct product is not in stock: the representative offers an alternative that will 'do the trick', without being completely certain that it is in fact suitable.

Once the purpose is known, it is then for the buyer to show he relies on the seller's skill *and* that it is reasonable to do so. In the typical retail sale, the mere fact that the buyer goes to the retailer is sufficient to indicate such reliance[25] but the seller can take steps to rebut the presumption. So, when the buyer asks whether the product can perform a certain function the seller can respond that he does not know, and suggest the buyer makes his own decision or takes independent advice. With certain products, such as complex machinery, the buyer may know more about the capabilities than the seller, particularly if he has collaborated in the design, which would make reliance on the seller's skill unreasonable. However, if the buyer places *some* reliance on the seller's skill, even though only partial, the seller may be liable.[26]

Seller's tactics:

● Do not enquire too closely as to the buyer's intended use.

● Offer only 'approved' parts, spares, modifications etc.

● Do not state or imply that the goods are suitable for unusual or non-approved purposes, modifications, fitting of accessories, methods of service or repair etc.

● If the buyer asks whether the goods will be suitable for a particular purpose and you are not sure, then either find out or admit you do not know. Suggest he makes his own evaluation or takes independent advice so that he will not then be relying on the seller's skill and judgment.

● If, having advised the buyer that the goods may not be suitable, he nevertheless insists on buying, then ensure he is fully aware of the limitations and dangers. Obtain written confirmation that he accepts the goods against your advice and with full knowledge of those limitations.

Buyer's tactics:

● Fully inform the seller of the intended use, even though it may appear obvious to you.

● In the case of raw materials and components which are to be manufactured into a finished product, ensure the supplier is aware of the processes that will be applied and the eventual operating conditions. Obtain his agreement that his components are suitable.

● Play the role of an idiot who knows nothing about the product, thereby placing reliance on the seller's skill to explain the method of use.

Sample

Sale of Goods Act 1979, s. 15(2):

In the case of a contract for sale by sample there is an implied condition —

(a) that the bulk will correspond with the sample in quality;

(b) that the buyer will have a reasonable opportunity of comparing the bulk with the sample;

(c) that the goods will be free from any defect, rendering them unmerchantable, which would not be apparent on reasonable examination of the sample.

To constitute a sale by sample, there has to be something more than a display of the goods and the buyer saying: 'I want one like that'. There must be an intention to deal on the basis of the sample shown.[27] Between retailers and consumers this is rare, except for items such as perfumes or carpets. Between businesses it is common, e.g., a component manufacturer providing a sample for testing and approval by the finished product manufacturer; he in turn trying to persuade retailers to stock it.

The temptation for the seller is to provide an above-average sample: the best rather than one which is truly representative of the bulk that will follow.[28] He might provide it in an ideal state, e.g. the sample sheet of material shown flat and smooth, without the sharp edges, folds, wrinkles etc. which are present on the bulk.[29] It might have features on it which the bulk lacks, e.g., the sample electrical appliance complete with a safety cut-out device which will not be on standard models.

Seller's tactics:

● Ensure the sample used is representative of the bulk that will be delivered, not the best example or with features not on those delivered.

● If there are likely to be differences, point this out at the time the sample is shown.

● Give the buyer ample opportunity to examine the sample so that he cannot later complain of defects that should have been apparent.

Buyer's tactics:

● Insist that the sample shown is to form the basis of the contract.

● If possible retain the sample for later comparison, or insist the seller does so.

● Beware of a quick examination of the sample.

STRICT LIABILITY FOR BREACH OF CONTRACT

Liability for breach of the terms implied by the Sale of Goods Act 1979, ss. 13 to 15, is *strict*, i.e., the *seller* of goods is liable even though he has taken every possible care and is not at fault[30]. A shop is liable for the quality of goods sold in boxes, cans etc. where the fault lies with the manufacturer and there is no way the shop could have detected it.

REMEDIES FOR BREACH OF CONTRACT

If the buyer (hirer etc.) suffers loss or injury as a consequence of a breach of contract, i.e., the goods being misdescribed, unmerchantable, unfit for purpose or otherwise breaching an express or implied term (e.g., late delivery) then he can claim damages for that loss.

The loss to be compensated must ensue as the direct and natural result, in the ordinary course of events, from the breach; or be in the reasonable contemplation of the parties as a probable result of the breach. This rule, established in *Hadley* v *Baxendale*,[31] presents difficulties of 'remoteness' when trying to establish what are natural or foreseeable losses, particularly in relation to financial losses for commercial buyers when the goods cannot be used or resold as intended.[32]

It is therefore possible to claim purely *financial losses* from a breach of contract, i.e., where no injury or physical damage has occurred. In this respect contract differs from the losses claimable for negligence and under the Consumer Protection Act 1987, where there must be some physical damage or injury (see chapters 3 and 4).

Where damage or injury does result, then this is claimable. The buyer is not limited to recovering the price of the goods or costs of their repair.[33]

Breach of the implied conditions may also enable the buyer to repudiate the contract and recover the purchase price. Thus if the goods supplied are not of merchantable quality the buyer can reject, get his money back and claim for consequential damage. He may *choose* to keep the goods and claim only damages. He is not obliged to accept a repair, replacement or credit note.

However, the right to reject may be lost once he has 'accepted' the goods, at which point he is limited to damages only. The precise point at which acceptance occurs is often difficult to determine and the rules provided by the Sale of Goods Act 1979, ss. 34 and 35 are none too helpful.[34] According to s. 35 acceptance can occur (*inter alia*) through expiration of time or by acting inconsistently with the seller's ownership, e.g., by continuing to use the goods or by attempting a repair. A buyer might inadvertently prejudice his rights if, on spotting a defect, he does not immediately reject the goods. Typically he will complain to the seller, agree to a repair, then other defects appear, further repairs, more defects until he gets fed up and demands his money back: then it may be too late to reject.[35]

The rules for, and effect of, acceptance are of no consequence where the claim is for loss or damage *caused by* the defective product. The buyer of contaminated food who is made seriously ill will not be too concerned whether he gets a price refund!

EXCLUSION CLAUSES AND THE BATTLE OF THE FORMS

The seller is restricted by the law in attempting to use exclusion or limitation clauses to avoid or reduce liability. These are statements on notices, in the small print of sales documents, invoices and so on, such as:

'No cash refunds on sale goods.'

'All defects must be reported within seven days.'

'Seller accepts no liability for loss or injury howsoever caused.'

'Our liability shall be limited to repair or replacement only.'

'Our liabilty for loss or injury shall not exceed £50,000 or the contract price, whichever is the greater.'

These may prove unenforceable if challenged.

The Unfair Contract Terms Act 1977 makes purported exclusion or limitation of liabilities for breach of the implied terms of description, sample, merchantability and fitness *unenforceable* in a sale *between a business and a private consumer*. Regulations issued under the Fair Trading Act 1973 also make the display of such clauses a *criminal offence.*[36]

Exclusion clauses in contracts between two businesses may, however, be enforceable provided they pass a 'reasonableness test'. The Act gives guide-lines[37] as to what is 'reasonable', one of the more important factors being the strength of bargaining position. So when a business negotiates to buy it may have the power to impose its own terms of purchase, to shop around for a better deal etc. In such cases the courts will hold that the business is strong enough to look after itself, so if it agrees to the seller's terms it will be bound by them.[38]

Attempts to exclude other legal liabilities, e.g., for negligence and for damage covered by the Consumer Protection Act 1987, may also be void (see chapters 3 and 4).

Seller's tactics:

● In a sale to a business buyer, incorporate clauses which have elements of reasonableness, e.g., rather than excluding liability completely, offer a limited amount such as the contract price or a maximum figure.[39]

● Offer alternative terms at different prices, e.g., at the lower price more onerous terms, but more generous terms for a higher price.[40]

In practice there are two problems:

(a) Hardly anyone bothers reading the terms, and if they did probably would not understand them.

(b) The 'battle of the forms': the buyer asks for a quotation using a form containing his terms and conditions; the seller offers a price on a form containing his contradicting terms; the buyer places an order back on the original terms; the seller accepts the order, and so on. Whose terms apply? The answer is not easy and, despite the countless occasions on which the problem must have occurred in commercial transactions, there is little case law and what there is does not make the position absolutely clear. Presumably most businesses sort it out between themselves without recourse to the courts.

The traditional approach of the courts is to view the communications according to common law rules of offer and acceptance. When an offer is made on certain terms, then an acceptance is valid only if it is on those terms. If any other terms are substituted then the purported 'acceptance' is in fact a counter-offer, to be accepted or rejected by the original offeror. If he then responds using the original terms, this is yet another counter-offer. Only when a set of terms is unconditionally agreed will there be a binding contract on those terms.

Some judges use the analogy of a military campaign, with the 'last shot' being decisive, but this is not invariably the outcome of the battle. It may be that earlier in the campaign one of the parties indicated his acceptance of the other's terms, so that any later communications (e.g., the final acknowledgement) are not effective. It can also be that the battle is never decided! The terms are irreconcilable, and have to be substituted by a 'reasonable implication'.[41]

In *Butler Machine Tool Co. Ltd* v *Ex-Cell-O Corporation (England) Ltd.*[42] the subject-matter was a machine tool. On 23 May 1969, in response to an inquiry by the buyer, the seller made a written quotation offering to supply it for £75,535, delivery in 10 months' time, subject to certain terms which 'shall prevail over any terms and conditions in the buyer's order'. These included a price variation clause, providing for the goods to be charged at the price ruling at the time of delivery. On 27 May the buyer replied by placing an order for the machine. This order contained terms which made no provision for any price variation. At the foot of the buyer's order was a tear off acknowledgement of receipt of the order stating 'We accept your order on the terms and conditions stated thereon'. On 5 June the seller signed this acknowledgement and returned it to the buyer together with a letter stating that the buyer's order was being entered in accordance with the seller's quotation of 23 May. On delivery of the machine the seller claimed that the price had increased by £2,892.

The Court of Appeal found that the buyer had not accepted the original offer of 23 May, but had made a counter-offer which the seller accepted. The seller's acknowledgement should therefore be regarded as an acceptance, not a further counter-offer to be accepted by the buyer taking delivery. The buyer's terms, with the fixed price, applied.

However, the circumstances of each case have to be looked at. The position under English law is far from satisfactory. The Uniform Commercial Code adopted by most American States offers a more satisfactory solution, as does the Uniform Law on the Formation of Contracts for the International Sale of Goods (ULFIS) which can be applied to international sales.

Buyer's tactics:

- Try to impose your terms of purchase on the seller. If he is reluctant to accept these, ask him why he insists on his terms. If he is seeking to exclude liabilities, does this mean he has no confidence in the quality of his product? Some arm-twisting might persuade him to concede: suggest to him that he has a high reputation to maintain, that he has been extolling the virtues of his product in advertising and in pre-contractual negotiations with you and yet here in the small print is saying he refuses to accept liability for poor quality. Would he like you to spread the word to other potential customers that here is a supplier who is not prepared to stand by his product?

- Perhaps the seller has never thought about the terms: they have always appeared on the back of his sales documents and never been challenged by a buyer. They were written by a lawyer years ago in legal jargon which no one has read, let alone understood. By pointing out to him what these terms actually mean he may be persuaded to change them.

- Point out to the seller that even though he might be able to exclude his liabilities under the contract of sale to you, he cannot as a producer exclude liability to victims of defects in his products (see chapter 3). He should therefore have adequate insurance or resources to cover such claims.

Tactics for sellers and buyers:

● Ensure the terms are adequately communicated before or at the time the contract is made. If they appear later they will not apply.[43]

● Ensure your terms are the ones that apply, i.e., that you win the battle of the forms.

● If you cannot be sure that you will you win the battle, then take the trouble to read the other party's terms. You may be able to change them, at least for future contracts.

With the new liabilities under the Consumer Protection Act 1987 it is even more important to provide for contractual recourse between the parties in the chain of supply. Previous lack of concern at whose terms are incorporated could prove expensive. Further tactics for buyers and sellers are discussed in later chapters.

WHO CAN SUE AND BE SUED FOR BREACH OF CONTRACT?

Only the *parties to the contract* can sue and be sued for breach of contract.

Liability for defective goods is primarily with the immediate supplier,[44] normally a shop or dealer rather than the manufacturer. In the context of employment this will not be the individual salesperson, but the employer on whose behalf he or she made the transaction.

That supplier is only liable in contract to the buyer (hirer or debtor) not third party victims.

This principle of 'privity of contract' can lead to absurd results. A man buys a new car; the brakes fail and he crashes; he could sue the dealer for breach of contract (the goods are not merchantable or fit for purpose). The dealer would be liable, even though the fault were in the manufacture of the brake components over which he had no control and which he could not be expected to discover during a pre-delivery check.

The owner could sue for the cost of repairs to the car or a refund of the purchase price. He could claim for injuries and consequential losses (hiring a replacement car, lost wages etc.). But the pedestrian who was run over when the brakes failed would have no *contractual* claim.

If the man's wife were driving at the time, she would have no contractual claim, unless they had bought the car on a joint basis.[45]

The seller (dealer), having been made contractually liable, could in turn claim his loss from the person from whom he bought the goods (the car manufacturer). The manufacturer could claim from the component supplier (brake manufacturer) whose defective part caused the crash.

But if anyone in the chain has gone out of business, or protected themselves by means of a valid exclusion clause, then the link is broken. Remember that the dealer cannot exclude his liabilities to a private purchaser, but between the businesses an exclusion clause may be enforceable if deemed reasonable. Businesses should therefore check carefully their terms of purchase so that they can get a full indemnity from their suppliers.

WHAT IS THE RELEVANCE OF CONTRACT NOW THAT THE CONSUMER PROTECTION ACT 1987 HAS BEEN IMPLEMENTED?

The Consumer Protection Act 1987 gives rights to victims of defective products which are not dependent on a contractual relationship, but:

(a)   it does not cover all types of product;

(b)   it is concerned with safety-related defects only;

(c)   it covers personal injury and damage to private property only, not other losses;

(d)   it makes 'producers' liable, whereas contract law applies to anyone in the distribution chain, such as retailers.

SUMMARY

The law of contract creates rights and duties for those who are parties to the contract. Through the implied terms of the Sale of Goods Act 1979 and similar statutes it provides excellent remedies for buyers, hirers etc., but is no use to third parties.

A seller can gain some protection by using the provisos within the implied terms and (in non-consumer sales) by reasonable exclusion clauses.

NOTES

1   For detailed coverage of the law of contract see any of the standard textbooks on the subject, e.g., *Anson's Law of Contract*, 26th ed. by A.G. Guest (Oxford: Clarendon Press, 1984); *Cheshire, Fifoot and Furmston's Law of Contract*, 11th ed. by M.P. Furmston (London: Butterworths, 1986); G.H. Treitel, *Law of Contract*, 7th ed. (London: Stevens & Sons, 1987).

2   Consumer Transactions (Restrictions on Statements) Order 1976 (SI 1976/1813 amended by SI 1978/127).

3   *Carlill* v *Carbolic Smoke Ball Co.* [1893] 1 QB 256; *Shanklin Pier Ltd.* v *Detel Products Ltd.* [1951] 2 KB 854.

4   But a guarantee cannot exclude liability for loss or damage which arises from goods proving defective while in consumer use, resulting from *negligence* by the manufacturer or distributor (Unfair Contract Terms Act 1977, s. 5).

5   Consumer Transactions (Restrictions on Statements) Order; see note 2.

6   Supply of Goods and Services Act 1982, ss. 1 to 9; Supply of Goods (Implied Terms) Act 1973, ss. 9 to 11 as substituted by Consumer Credit Act 1974, sch. 4, para. 35.

7   See D.K. Allen, *Misrepresentation* (London: Sweet & Maxwell, 1988).

8   *Arcos Ltd.* v *E.A. Ronaasen & Son* [1933] AC 470

9   For example, *Grenfell* v *E.B. Meyrowitz Ltd* [1936] 2 All ER 1313. *Reardon Smith Line Ltd.* v *Hansen-Tangen* [1976] 1 WLR 989.

10   Unfair Contract Terms Act 1977, sch. 2; *Photo Production Ltd* v *Securicor Transport Ltd* [1980] AC 827. See below for other cases on exclusion clauses.

11   Sale of Goods Act 1979, s. 61.

12   *Geddling* v *Marsh* [1920] 1 KB 668; *Aswan Engineering Establishment Co.* v *Lupdine Ltd* [1987] 1 WLR 1.

13   *Wormell* v *RHM Agriculture (East) Ltd* [1987] 1 WLR 1091.

14   Working Paper No. 85 on the Sale and Supply of Goods (London: HMSO, 1983), which proposes the introduction of a more satisfactory definition, including a notion of durability.

15   The draft Sale and Supply of Goods Bill (Law Com. No. 160, Cm 137) proposes an improved definition, based on 'acceptable quality'. This will include factors such as durability, safety, appearance and finish.

16   See any of the standard texts on sale of goods, e.g., P.S. Atiyah, *The Sale of Goods*, 7th ed. (London: Pitman, 1985).

17   *Bartlett v Sydney Marcus Ltd* [1965] 1 WLR 1013.

18   *Crowther v Shannon Motor Co.* [1975] 1 WLR 30.

19   *B.S. Brown & Son Ltd v Craiks Ltd* [1970] 1 WLR 752.

20   *Godley v Perry* [1960] 1 WLR 9; *Lee v York Coach & Marine* [1977] RTR 35.

21   *Millars of Falkirk Ltd. v Turpie* [1976] SLT 66.

22   See M. Whincup, 'A new deal for consumers' (1988) 138 NLJ 7.

23   *H. Parsons (Livestock) Ltd v Uttley Ingham & Co. Ltd* [1978] QB 791; *B.S. Brown & Son Ltd v Craiks Ltd* [1970] 1 WLR 752.

24   *Griffiths v Peter Conway Ltd* [1939] 1 All ER 685.

25   *Grant v Australian Knitting Mills Ltd* [1936] AC 85.

26   *Cammell Laird & Co. Ltd v Manganese Bronze & Brass Co. Ltd* [1934] AC 402.

27   *James Drummond & Sons v E. H. Van Ingen & Co.* (1887) 12 App Cas 284.

28   *Champanhac & Co. Ltd v Waller & Co. Ltd* [1948] 2 All ER 724.

29   *E. & S. Ruben Ltd. v Faire Brothers & Co. Ltd* [1949] 1 KB 254.

30   Similarly for other forms of supply of goods under associated statutes. See note 6.

31   (1854) 9 Exch 341. The Sale of Goods Act 1979, ss. 50, 51 and 53, embody this rule.

32   *Victoria Laundry (Windsor) Ltd* v *Newman Industries Ltd* [1949] 2 KB 528; *C. Czarnikow Ltd* v *Koufos* [1969] 1 AC 350; *H. Parsons (Livestock) Ltd* v *Uttley Ingham & Co. Ltd* [1978] QB 791. For a general discussion, see H. McGregor, *McGregor On Damages,* 15th ed. (London: Sweet & Maxwell, 1988) or the leading textbooks on contract cited in note 1.

33   *Godley* v *Perry* [1960] 1 WLR 9; *Grant* v *Australian Knitting Mills Ltd* [1936] AC 85; *H. Parsons (Livestock) Ltd* v *Uttley Ingham & Co. Ltd* [1978] QB 791.

34   The draft Sale and Supply of Goods Bill (Law Com. No. 160, Cm 137) contains new provisions on acceptance.

35   *Bernstein* v *Pamson Motors (Golders Green) Ltd* [1987] 2 All ER 220; *Farnworth Finance Facilities Ltd* v *Attryde* [1970] 1 WLR 1053; *Laurelgates Ltd* v *Lombard North Central Ltd* (1983) 133 NLJ 720.

36   See note 2.

37   Unfair Contract Terms Act 1977, sch. 2.

38   *Photo Production Ltd* v *Securicor Transport Ltd* [1980] AC 827; *George Mitchell (Chesterhall) Ltd* v *Finney Lock Seeds Ltd* [1983] 2 AC 803. For a general survey of the cases, see the standard texts on contract.

39   *R.W. Green Ltd.* v *Cade Bros Farms* [1978] 1 Lloyd's Rep 602.

40   *Woodman* v *Photo Trade Processing Ltd* (1981) unreported. Text of the judgment of Exeter County Court set out in C.J. Miller and B.W. Harvey, *Consumer and Trading Law: Cases and Materials,* (London: Butterworths, 1985).

41   Per Lord Denning MR in *Butler Machine Tool Co. Ltd* v *Ex-Cell-O Corporation (England) Ltd* [1979] 1 WLR 401.

42   [1979] 1 WLR 401. See also *British Road Services Ltd* v *Arthur V. Crutchley & Co. Ltd* [1968] 1 All ER 811.

43   *Olley* v *Marlborough Court Ltd* [1949] 1 All ER 127.

44   For certain types of credit agreements the Consumer Credit Act 1974, s. 75, makes both the supplier of the goods and the creditor (e.g., bank or finance house) jointly and severally liable.

45   *Preist* v *Last* [1903] 2 KB 148.

3

Civil Liability under Part I of the Consumer Protection Act 1987

Part I of the Consumer Protection Act ('CPA') 1987, implemented 1st March 1988, is Britain's response to an EEC Directive[1] designed to harmonise product liability law throughout the Community. It gives improved rights to victims of defective products bringing a civil action.

Parts II to V introduce new criminal offences and extend the powers of enforcement authorities. These will be considered in chapter 5.

The draft Directive was first circulated in the mid 1970s and, following much debate and amendment, finally adopted in a compromise form in 1985. Each member State was then required to implement legislation to give effect to its provisions by July 1988. Complete harmonisation has not been initially achieved because such was the controversy over three particular issues that the only way forward was to allow individual member States a choice by way of derogation from certain provisions. These are the inclusion of a so-called 'development risks defence', whether agricultural produce should be exempted, and whether there should be a financial ceiling on the amount of damages payable.

This means that there will be different laws in certain member States, which could give rise to forum shopping by a plaintiff to find the most favourable jurisdiction in which to pursue a defendant. There will be a review of the derogations after a seven-year transition period in 1995 to try to achieve full harmonisation.

A Directive sets out guiding principles in the form of 'Articles', together with an explanatory preamble. The detailed legislation passed by individual member States must 'give effect' to these principles, but the interpretation and wording may be slightly different.

CPA 1987, s. 1(1), states:

> This Part shall have effect for the purpose of making such provision as is necessary in order to comply with the product liability Directive and shall be construed accordingly.

Thus in interpreting CPA 1987 the judges can refer to the Directive, which should take precedence in the event of conflict.

Article 1 of the Directive states the basic principle:

> The producer shall be liable for damage caused by a defect in his product.

The two most significant things about this provision have to be deduced from what it does not say:

(a)   There is no need for a contractual relationship.

(b)   There is no need to establish fault.

Strict liability becomes a basis on which a victim can sue a producer.

The burden of proof is still on the victim to show the damage, the defect and the causal link between them, but he now has a much better chance of success because he does not have to establish negligence. If the victim is a buyer (hirer etc.) then he already has a strict liability claim against the seller (supplier) in contract, so the advantages of CPA 1987 are not so great. However, he now has an equal or better chance of success against producers, which will be of benefit when the immediate seller is unable to pay for the damage.

This has far-reaching implications for a producer. Unless he can use the very limited defences provided by CPA 1987, if his product is defective and causes damage (as defined) then he will be liable — simple as that. Taking reasonable care is not a defence.

Furthermore he cannot limit or exclude liability by any contract term, notice or otherwise (CPA 1987, s. 7).

This basic concept of strict liability could come as a shock to many producers, particularly those not exporting to the USA or other jurisdictions with established strict liability regimes and therefore not familiar with the legal exposure. Claims against producers will inevitably increase, as will the cost of insurance cover. However, there are further implications which will be examined in this chapter by taking the following elements in turn:

(a)   Who is liable?

(b)   What is a product?

(c)   What is a defect?

(d)   What type of damage is covered?

(e)   Time-limits for bringing an action.

(f)   What defences are available?

(g)   Choice of jurisdiction: forum shopping.

WHO IS LIABLE?

The intention of the Directive was to give a wide meaning to the term 'producer' to try to ensure that a victim had an easily identifiable target against whom to pursue an action, and then leave it to those in the chain of manufacture and supply to sort out among themselves how much each of them should contribute.

CPA 1987 implements this principle by defining 'producer' in the limited sense of actual manufacturer or processor of the product, but then extends potential liability to three other categories of persons who are not involved in any manufacturing but may be treated *as if* producers:

(a)   Own-branders.

(b)   Importers.

(c)   Suppliers who cannot trace the product back to the actual producer.

It is necessary to set out the full text of CPA 1987, s. 2, to explore its implications:

(1)   Subject to the following provisions of this Part, where any damage is caused wholly or partly by a defect in a product, every person to whom subsection (2) below applies shall be liable for the damage.

(2)   This subsection applies to —

   (a)   the producer of the product;

   (b)   any person who, by putting his name on the product or using a trade mark or other distinguishing mark in relation to the product, has held himself out to be the producer of the product;

   (c)   any person who has imported the product into a member State from a place outside the member States in order, in the course of any business of his, to supply it to another.

(3)   Subject as aforesaid, where any damage is caused wholly or partly by a defect in a product, any person who supplied the product (whether to the person who suffered the damage, to the producer of any product in which the product in question is comprised or to any other person) shall be liable for the damage if —

   (a)   the person who suffered the damage requests the supplier to identify one or more of the persons (whether still in existence or not) to whom subsection (2) above applies in relation to the product;

   (b)   that request is made within a reasonable period after the damage occurs and at a time when it is not reasonably practicable for the person making the request to identify all those persons; and

   (c)   the supplier fails, within a reasonable period after receiving the request, either to comply with the request or to identify the person who supplied the product to him.

(4)   Neither subsection (2) nor subsection (3) above shall apply to a person in respect of any defect in any game or agricultural produce if the only supply of the game or produce by that person to another was at a time when it had not undergone an industrial process.

(5)   Where two or more persons are liable by virtue of this Part for the same damage, their liability shall be joint and several.

(6)   This section shall be without prejudice to any liability arising otherwise than by virtue of this Part.

Subsection (6) can be conveniently dealt with first: CPA 1987 does not destroy any rights a victim may have under the law of contract, negligence or other torts — it adds to those rights.

Liability primarily rests under s. 2(2)(a) with a 'producer'.

Who is a 'producer'?

By CPA 1987, s. 1(2):

. . . 'producer', in relation to a product, means —

(a)   the person who manufactured it;

(b)   in the case of a substance which has not been manufactured but has been won or abstracted, the person who won or abstracted it;

(c)   in the case of a product which has not been manufactured, won or abstracted but essential characteristics of which are attributable to an industrial or other process having been carried out (for example, in relation to agricultural produce), the person who carried out that process.

'Person' in the context of employment means the employer (usually a company), not the individual employee who carried out the operation or transaction.

Paragraph (a) of the definition of 'producer' seems simple enough but in fact creates a number of grey areas which will only be sorted out by test cases. It is regrettable that the word 'manufactured' is not defined. What about someone who purely assembles components made by others, mixes ingredients, or installs a unit supplied in kit form? The Directive provides some clarification:

'Producer' means the manufacturer of a *finished* product, the producer of any raw material or the manufacturer of a *component part* (Art. 3(1), emphasis added).

An *assembler* of a finished product made entirely from bought-in components therefore is a producer, because he has incorporated these into his manufactured product. He is liable for defects in those components, even though:

(a)   He could not have detected them.

(b)   He has no control over the component manufacturer's design or production process.

(c)   The component manufacturer's name or logo appears on the component.

(d)   The defect in the component was the sole cause of the damage.

The component manufacturer is *also* a producer, and generally would pay in full for the damage caused by his defective component. Thus there are two producers. The great advantage of this for the victim is that if one of these cannot pay, the other will: this is the 'deep pocket' provided by the principle of joint and several liability.

An *installer* will probably not be regarded as a producer, because he does not manufacture a product as such, but merely supplies a service in relation to someone else's product. So, someone fitting a door into a frame in a house would presumably not be liable for defects in the door itself (unless he caused them during fitting); similarly the car dealer who fits a tow bar on a new car would not thereby manufacture a product. But where someone modifies the characteristics of a product, e.g., converting a standard car into a high-performance version by replacing and adding various parts, he might become a producer. Similarly building a central heating unit from unrelated components rather than assembling a complete kit. The dividing line may prove hard to define.

Particular concern has been expressed about pharmacists, doctors and other health care personnel who mix medicinal ingredients into a prescription. By the principles outlined above, they could be liable as producers. For NHS staff, the producer would be the Health Authority. However, many medical practitioners are not employees, but self-employed and under contract to an authority. Like pharmacists, they would need to keep careful records of the sources of drugs to be able to pass on liability to the manufacturer responsible for any defect.

We await court decisions to clarify the meaning of 'manufactured'. Meanwhile those who assemble, mix, convert or install products could adopt policies which indicate they are not in the 'manufacturing' business:

● Obtain full instructions from the actual manufacturers and follow these precisely.

● Get parts delivered in completely prefabricated form, so no modification occurs on fitting.

● Market themselves as installers of other manufacturers' products.

Printers and others concerned with producing information in books, records, tapes etc., where mistakes could result in defective instructions or warnings, might also be deemed producers. It is thought that if they faithfully reproduce errors in the material provided to them, they will not be held liable. If they are responsible for a printing error then liability would depend on negligence, rather than strict liability under CPA 1987.[2]

No mention is made anywhere in the Act of computer software. There seems little doubt that the manufacturer of a machine which is rendered unsafe due to defective software incorporated into it would be liable for producing a defective machine, but what of the actual software producer? Is software a 'product'? The chip, tape or other medium on which information is stored would be a product, so a physical defect in that medium should be covered. Difficulties arise where the defect is in the logic or the instructions put into it, i.e., an intellectual rather than a physical defect. The distinction, if there is to be one, could be extremely difficult to make. Until case law clarifies the position, creators of software would be wise to assume that they are within the definition of 'producer'.

The second paragraph of the definition of 'producer' covers those who mine or otherwise collect products such as coal, gas, oil or clay. The process of abstraction makes them producers.

Paragraph (c) covers processors and refiners. The process must alter the characteristics of the product, so purely packing or cleaning someone else's product does not amount to a process. This is particularly significant for food processors because primary agricultural produce is exempt, but once it has undergone an industrial process it becomes the liability of the processor, not the grower.

Own-branders

By s. 2(2)(b) an own-brander (such as a department store or supermarket) becomes one of those liable if, but only if, he held himself out as producer of that product.

The CPA 1987 is not clear about what constitutes holding out. Presumably it will depend on how the branding is perceived by the reasonable consumer. So, if the *only* name or logo appearing on the product is the own-brander's then he is liable. In fact most own-branded products have some indication, often in very small print, that someone else is the manufacturer.

Let us examine some typical examples, using 'Smiths' as the brand name prominently appearing on the product or its packaging:

● 'Made for Smiths Ltd by Jones Ltd' or 'A product of Jones Ltd' would seem to exempt Smiths. The consumer has been informed that Smiths Ltd is not the producer. But how prominently need this be shown?

● 'Specially made for Smiths Ltd', or 'Packed for Smiths Ltd' with no manufacturer's name shown, also seems to indicate that Smiths Ltd is not the manufacturer, so provided, it could identify the actual manufacturer (see s. 2(3) below) it again should escape.

● 'Smiths' or 'Smiths genuine approved parts' on the packaging, with the actual manufacturer's name on the product itself. Smiths Ltd could again argue that it has not given the impression of being producer, but is this what the consumer perceives?

If there is no indication at all on the product or packaging other than the Smiths name or logo, then it appears to be no defence for Smiths Ltd to say: 'Everybody knows we don't actually make the product'.

Thus a company putting its name on pens, promotional gifts etc., even though it might be a hotel, finance house or other blatantly obviously non-manufacturing organisation, can presumably be liable for defects. Similarly there seems no reason why an individual, such as a television or football personality, who endorses a product cannot be held liable. When the Bill was going through the House of Lords, concern was raised about a pharmacist putting his name on a bottle of pills manufactured by a drug company. Their lordships concluded that this would not amount to holding himself out as producer, but such situations have yet to be tested in court.

Until the courts clarify the position, own-branders would be wise to ensure that there is a clear and prominent indication that someone else is the producer, preferably by naming him. This should appear at any place where the brand name or logo appears, i.e., on the product, its labels, packaging, advertising and promotional literature. Failing this, the own-brander should ensure that the producer can be traced and brought in as a joint defendant, and that he has adequate resources and insurance cover to pay damages.

Importers

By s. 2(2)(c) an importer of a product from *outside* the EEC is treated as a producer. The intention is that victims do not have to pursue claims against distant manufacturers in countries which may have less favourable laws. Once within the EEC an import into one member State from another is not affected. Thus a defective Japanese product imported into Germany and then into England where it causes damage will render the German importer liable. The German importer can then seek recourse back to the Japanese exporter on his contract, but that is his problem, not the victim's.

The supplier who cannot identify the producer

Generally a supplier (retailer, distributor, installer etc.) will not be liable under CPA 1987, Part I, for defective products (though he may be liable in contract or negligence, or criminally liable under CPA 1987 Part II). Most products are traceable back to the producer because they have his name or other identification mark on them, or they are of a unique design. A supplier only becomes liable under s. 2(3) where the product is 'anonymous' (e.g., fasteners, sheet materials, fluids, chemicals etc. with no markings or unique characteristics) or is so badly damaged in the accident that it cannot be identified, *and* he has no other means of tracing that product back to his supplier, e.g., purchasing records showing that it was part of a batch which came from a particular supplier.

The supplier need not identify the actual manufacturer, just the next person back up the chain of supply. Each supplier can pass the buck until it reaches the producer, own-brander or EC importer.

Joint and several liability

With many manufactured products there will be a number of separate producers in the chain, supplying in turn raw materials, sub-components, components and the final product. Any manufacturer downstream of a defect who incorporates it into his product becomes liable as one of the producers. A car manufacturer is therefore liable for a defect in the tyre, windscreen, brakes etc. supplied to him by an entirely separate manufacturer.

Joint and several liability means that where there are two or more persons liable for the defect the victim can sue any or all of those persons. He may simply choose the most conspicuous and deep-pocketed as an attractive target. That defendant can join any co-producers in the defence or seek contribution from them,[3] but this will be of little comfort if they have gone out of business or are not worth pursuing.

In a situation where a component is to blame for an accident, e.g., a defective car windscreen shatters and injures the occupants, it is likely that the victim will pursue a claim against both the windscreen and car manufacturers. Ultimately the windscreen manufacturer will pay, unless:

(a) he cannot pay through lack of resources or insurance, or he has meanwhile gone out of business; or

(b) in his contract of supply to the car manufacturer he incorporated a clause limiting liability to a certain figure or excluding it altogether.

(a) has enormous implications: a producer buying in raw materials and components, or an own-brander buying finished products, should be very wary of purchasing from small or under-insured manufacturers, or those whose future financial viability looks doubtful. It might be preferable to pay a higher price for similar, or even inferior, products from a manufacturer who has the resources, insurance and greater likelihood of staying in businesss to pay his share of any liability.

Bad news indeed for the small manufacturer.

(b) makes it essential to check the terms of the contract of supply, and renegotiate as necessary.

By CPA 1987, s. 7, liability to *victims* cannot be excluded or limited by any such terms. However, in the contracts between businesses in the production and distribution chains the clauses may be enforceable[4] in establishing how much each one finally contributes to the damages. If windscreen producer W supplies car producer C on the condition that its liability for any damage caused by defects shall not exceed £50,000, this cannot prevent a victim suing W for a higher amount, but W could then join C in the defence or seek contribution from him for all but the agreed £50,000. If the victim instead sues C, then C will only recover up to £50,000 from W.

Negotiating more favourable terms may prove difficult with the larger suppliers, who might adopt a take-it-or-leave-it approach, i.e., they will only supply on their terms. While the Unfair Contract Terms Act 1977 provides a reasonableness test for the enforceability of terms between businesses (see chapter 2), cases brought under that Act suggest the courts are reluctant to intervene unless the terms are blatantly unfair and imposed by the very strong on the very weak. As Lord Wilberforce has commented:[5]

> . . . in commercial matters generally, when the parties are not of unequal bargaining power, and when risks are normally borne by insurance, . . . there is everything to be said . . . for leaving the parties free to apportion the risks as they think fit and for respecting their decisions.

Bad news for the small purchaser.

Section 2(1) makes any of the persons within the liability net potentially *fully* liable for damage caused *wholly or partly* by the defective product. However, the existing laws of contributory negligence (the victim being partly responsible) and civil contribution (other persons partly responsible) still operate to enable the defendant to offset part of his liability (see chapter 4).

Tactics for potential defendants

(a) *Check the traceability of products and their constituent parts: can suppliers and purchasers be identified?*

If not then liability cannot be properly apportioned. Tracing a defective part is easy when it is marked with a producer's name, part number etc., or is a unique design or is single-sourced, but is difficult with anonymous products which could have come from a number of sources. It is then only by adequate purchasing and sales records and material control systems that the producer who bought in the products can identify the source, and conversely the supplier can prove whether he did or did not supply the defective one in question. Consider:

● Marking, coding, colouring or otherwise putting an identifying characteristic on safety-related parts.

● Single sourcing.

● Strict material control: stock rotation systems; separate bins for products from separate suppliers; completely emptying one bin before starting on the next; recording 'cut-in' dates when one supplier's parts were substituted by another's.

● Maintaining records: liability can extend for up to 10 years (see page 55). For how long do you keep your purchasing or sales or material control records? Without these how can you prove who supplied the defective product?

  (b) *Ensure the financial viability of co-producers.*

● Check their capital, assets, published accounts, general trading performance (a company search is easily available).

● Help them achieve viability by long-term contracts, collaborative ventures, injections of capital, guarantees of loans etc.

● In the case of a group of companies, check whether you are in fact dealing with the large, financially sound parent company or a subsidiary with small assets. There is nothing to prevent a company from incorporating a subsidiary to carry on a particular part of its business. So when ABC Ltd develops a new, potentially dangerous product it could form ABC (Special Products) Ltd as a wholly owned subsidiary, with £100 share capital, lending it necessary resources to manufacture and market the product. ABC (Special Products) Ltd, as a separate legal person, is the producer and therefore liable for defects, but is only worth £100. ABC Ltd, is simply a shareholder, and by the principle of limited liability can only lose its £100. It would simply put the subsidiary company into liquidation when higher damages were assessed against it. (For further discussion of this tactic see pages 178–80.)

  The way round this as a purchaser of ABC's products is first to check the company structure (by a search if necessary) and then insist that the parent company backs the subsidiary by guarantees and insurance.

● Are they adequately insured? If not insist they increase cover. It may be possible to help by negotiating with one's own insurers to offer them a favourable policy.

  (c) *Ensure the contract of supply allows for proper recourse.*

The terms in the contracts between producers, own-branders and importers may contain clauses limiting or excluding liability.

The EC importer will also wish to recover any damages he had to pay from the exporter.

So:

● Check contractual terms; read the small print.

● Challenge and renegotiate as necessary.

● When importing, make the contract subject to English Law.

(d) *For own-branders:*

● Consider whether own-branding is a wise policy. Do the marketing benefits outweigh the potential legal exposure?

● Ensure that there is a clear indication on the product, labelling, packaging etc. that you are not the manufacturer.

● If the actual manufacturer's name is not shown, ensure you can identify him.

(e) *For suppliers:*

● As a seller you have liabilities under the Sale of Goods Act 1979 (see chapter 2) for defective products, but you could suggest to a buyer that he now has better legal rights against producers, so sue them instead and go for a deeper pocket than yours.

● Check traceability, both of anonymous goods and others which could be unidentifiable after an accident. Once you have identified your supplier it does not matter if he cannot pay or has gone out of business. You are no longer liable under CPA 1987, Part I, so the victims could lose out. Remember, however, that you may still be liable in contract, negligence or under CPA 1987, Part II.

WHAT IS A PRODUCT?

'Product' is defined in CPA 1987, s. 1(2), as 'any goods or electricity and . . . includes a product which is comprised in another product, whether by virtue of being a component part or raw material or otherwise'.

'Goods', by s. 45(1), includes substances (which can be natural or artificial, solid, liquid, gaseous or in the form of a vapour), things comprised in land by virtue of being attached to it (but not land itself), ships, aircraft and vehicles.

To be liable for a defective product a person must 'supply' that product to another in the course of his business (see 'Defences' below).

All manufactured and processed goods supplied by a business are therefore included, together with the raw materials and component parts incorporated into them. So too are gas, water and electricity. With electricity there must be a defect at the time of generation, so damage caused by disruptions in the supply through breakdowns in the distribution system are not covered.[6]

Waste can also be a product, certainly where it is sold as a by-product and probably also when the producer gives it away or pays someone to dispose of it. But if it is simply a discharge, then the producer will not be liable under CPA 1987, Part I, because it has not been 'supplied',[7] though he may face liability elsewhere.[8]

Not included are 'immovables', i.e., land, buildings and fixed structures such as bridges and roads. However, the building materials themselves are products, so if the bricks are defective and the house falls down there could be a claim. If it is the design or method of construction that is defective, then CPA 1987 does not apply. Problems of interpretation will inevitably arise with such things as oil-rigs, mobile homes on a permanent site and other borderline 'immovables'. Clearly items fitted into immovables, such as boilers, appliances, furniture etc. are covered.

Services are not products, so the provision of advice, information or know-how without any physical product is not included. Warnings and instructions accompanying the product are relevant to the meaning of 'defective'. Whether computer software is a product or service is debatable.

Specifically exempted are agricultural produce and game that has not gone through an industrial process. Agricultural produce is defined in s. 1(2) as 'any produce of the soil, of stock-farming or of fisheries'. Produce may be grown or reared by totally artificial methods, and probably 'soil' will not be regarded as an essential growing medium, so that vegetables grown in other cultures are exempt. Animals can be injected during their life with hormones which later cause damage to consumers, yet the farmer and hormone producer escape liability under CPA 1987, Part I. Chickens can be given salmonella-infected feed and reared in conditions which encourage spread of the infection, yet liability to consumers suffering food poisoning from eggs depends on proof of negligence or breach of some other statutory provision.

The rationale for this is that farmers, fishermen etc. should not be strictly liable for defects beyond their control, such as natural infestations, pollution and the long-term effects of fertilisers etc., whereas those involved in processing can make tests and devise methods of eliminating dangers. So a fisherman is not liable under Part I for selling fish contaminated during its life by chemical pollutants, but the fish processor would be.

It is not yet clear how much processing is required: potatoes in a natural state would be exempt, but not crisps; apples, but not apple pies; whole plaice, not breaded plaice; but what about filleted plaice? Normal harvesting, cleaning and packing on the farm or trawler is not an industrial process because it does not change the essential characteristics of the product. Canning, freezing, heat-treating and converting into processed food does, but what of the farmer who cleans, shreds, mixes and packs several varieties of vegetable to produce fresh vegetable salad, or the trawler skipper who freezes his catch to keep it fresh for later processing?

WHAT IS A DEFECT?

By CPA 1987, s. 3, a product is defective when it does not provide the safety which persons generally are entitled to expect, taking into account all the circumstances.

'Defective' is therefore limited to the safety of the product. Purely shoddy products, which may be unmerchantable or unfit for their purpose, but otherwise safe, are not within the definition and remedies will have to be sought under the law of contract.

The defect must also be the cause of personal injury or physical damage. A car with a defective engine may break down on the motorway, which is dangerous, but if the only consequence is a costly towing-off, that is not covered.

'Safety' is in terms of consumer expectation. Many products are, by their very nature, dangerous. Others can be dangerous if misused. Some products could be made safer if enough money were spent on them, or the design aimed at ultimate safety to the detriment of style and practicality. That does not necessarily make them defective.

The test is objective, i.e., what persons generally are entitled to expect, rather than the individual who has particular sensitivities.

Particular problems arise with medicinal products and adverse reactions to them. The more active the medicine, and the greater its potential benefits, the greater are the chances of adverse effects. When treating life-threatening conditions the medicine is likely to be more powerful than for less serious conditions, and the safety expectations therefore lower.

Section 3 requires the court to take all the circumstances into account, including three matters set out in paragraphs (a), (b) and (c) of s. 3(2).

> (a)   the manner in which, and purposes for which, the product has been marketed, its get-up, the use of any mark in relation to the product and any instructions for, or warnings with respect to, doing or refraining from doing anything with or in relation to the product.

The way the product is marketed has the most immediate impact on the public's expectation. Advertising, packaging, labelling, instructions for use, warnings, marks (such as BS kite marks), brochures, service manuals, correspondence and the actual words and gestures used in relation to the product all have an effect. Instructions and warnings must be provided when the danger is not obvious, covering both what to do and what not to do. Just how far these should go is discussed in chapter 6.

Tactics for producers are the same as described in chapter 2 regarding description, merchantability and fitness. In particular:

- Be accurate with information about the product.

- Do not exaggerate.

- Provide full warnings and instructions.

- Point out any limitations.

> (b)   what might reasonably be expected to be done with or in relation to the product.

This does not simply mean what the product is designed to do, but what the producer should reasonably foresee might be done, i.e., predictable misuse. Child-proof tops on bottles are an example. The prime duty is to design out the hazard, but if this is not feasible then adequate warnings or instructions must be provided (see chapter 6).

> (c)   the time when the product was supplied by its producer to another.

As technology and standards change, so does the public expectation. A car with a rigid steering column, cable-operated brakes and no seat-belts would be considered defective if so designed today, but 60 years ago such features were acceptable. Section 3(2) provides for this by adding:

> and nothing in this section shall require a defect to be inferred from the fact alone that the safety of a product which is supplied after that time is greater than the safety of the product in question.

Without this provision, producers would constantly have to recall and modify older products every time they introduced a safety improvement.

What is the precise time to which reference should be made: when designed, manufactured or actually sold? Section 4(2) states it is when the person 'supplied the product to another', the person being one of those defined in s. 2(2), i.e., producer, own-brander or EC importer. Thus for a product designed in 1985, manufactured in 1988, supplied to a distributor in 1989, sold in 1990 and causing damage in 1991 the relevant date is 1989. Products in storage pending delivery, or components awaiting assembly into finished products, could therefore become 'defective' if expectations meanwhile change, so may have to be modified or withdrawn. When legislation forces a change, adequate notice of the implementation date is invariably given.

Where there are several producers, the relevant time for each one is when he supplied it on to the next. This has implications for time-limits in bringing an action (see page 55).

The problem for many producers is the long period required to introduce a new or revised product. A safer method becomes apparent, but cannot be immediately adopted because of design, testing, procurement and manufacturing lead times. Meanwhile an increasingly outdated product is still being supplied. Consumers can only expect the producer to do what is practicable, not to stop production meanwhile. Producers cannot ignore the new method, nor expect consumers to keep waiting until it is convenient to introduce it, on the basis that 'We've always been making them like this and nobody ever complained'. The longer the production run in the face of changing expectations, the more likely the product will become regarded as defective.

Particularly difficult is the position of a producer who introduces a new, safer model while still producing older designs. That new model does not automatically make the old one defective, but the producer is himself changing the public's expectations, particularly with any advertising extolling the virtues of the new. His marketing strategy should carefully avoid implying that the older version is unsafe: it is safe enough by current standards.

A similar problem occurs when he begins to fit as standard a safety feature that was previously optional, or only previously offered by other producers. Suppose a car manufacturer in 1989 incorporates such a feature into current models. There is no legal requirement for it. Later the driver of a 1988 model has an accident which is partly attributable to the lack of that safety feature. Here the 1988 model is not defective, because consumer expectations in 1988 were not such as to require a car to be fitted with this feature, and incorporation of it into later models does not of itself make earlier versions defective.

To be able to refute allegations that his product was defective at the time, a producer could regularly put on file a state-of-the-art checklist, with accompanying documents and cross-references. This should list the features which are incorporated at a particular time both into his products and similar ones from other producers, as well as the technology available to test and eliminate defects. This could include regulations, BSI and other current standards. So, when an allegation is made that one of his products manufactured, say, nine years ago was not up to consumer expectations at that time, he has available evidence to prove otherwise. This relatively simple expedient, perhaps done on an annual basis, would avoid having to rely on memory or find and sift through old documents and publications.

WHAT TYPE OF DAMAGE IS COVERED?

CPA 1987, s. 5(1), provides:

> Subject to the following provisions of this section, in this Part 'damage' means death or personal injury or any loss of or damage to any property (including land).

Purely financial loss is not covered. If the product simply breaks, fails to perform or is substandard, without causing injury or property damage, then a claim could be made in contract, but not under CPA 1987.

Death and personal injury

The damages recoverable are as in any other civil cases, including compensation for the pain, suffering or impairment caused and the financial loss resulting from the death or injury. Personal injury includes 'any disease and any other impairment of a person's physical or mental condition' (s. 45(1)), and pre-natal injury (s. 6(3)).

Damage to property

Liability for damage to property is subject to three significant exceptions provided by s. 5(2), (3) and (4).

(a) *Damage to the product itself.*

(2) A person shall not be liable . . . for the loss of or any damage to the product itself or for the loss of or any damage to the whole or any part of any product which has been supplied with the product in question comprised in it.

If an electrical appliance catches fire due to an internal defect, then damage to that appliance cannot be recovered under CPA 1987. The buyer can pursue a claim under the Sale of Goods Act 1979 for his money back or other settlement.

If the fire were caused by a defective plug (manufactured by A) which was then fitted on the appliance (manufactured by B) *as original equipment*, then damage caused to the appliance by the defective plug would not be covered. However, if the appliance is sold without a plug, which has to be bought as a separate item and fitted on by the buyer, then the plug and appliance are separate products: damage caused to the appliance by the defective plug could be claimed. Similarly, a claim could be made if the plug had been purchased as a replacement for the original.

Remember also that if the plug were fitted as original equipment, then there are two producers, A and B, jointly and severally liable for injury or damage caused to *other* property. For the plug bought separately, A alone is fully liable.

The combined effect of these two rules might be to tempt producers to supply products in incomplete form: the plugs, batteries, connections, extra ingredients etc. all vital to make the thing usable having to be bought after the 'basic' product is supplied. The marketing consequences of adopting such tactics have to be weighed against the liability advantages: e.g., losing sales to competitors who provide the 'complete' product, or who fit as standard certain features which are 'extras' on your version.

(b) *Damage to business property.*

(3) A person shall not be liable . . . for any loss of or damage to any property which, at the time it is lost or damaged, is not —

(a)   of a description of property ordinarily intended for private use, occupation or consumption; and

(b)   intended by the person suffering the loss or damage mainly for his own private use, occupation or consumption.

If a defective electrical appliance damages a private house, then that loss can be claimed, but not if it burns down a factory. If the house is owned by a landlord who rents it to tenants, then the landlord cannot claim because he is not using the house mainly for his private occupation.

Damage caused to a private car by a defective accessory or replacement part can be claimed, but if that same part damages an identical car belonging to a company it cannot. Similarly if damage is caused to a heavy goods vehicle, even if that vehicle belonged to an enthusiast as part of a private collection, it cannot be claimed because that would be a type of property not ordinarily intended for private use.

Producers who supply products solely for business use, where the only likely consequence of a defect is damage to business property or financial loss, are therefore unaffected by CPA 1987, Part I. The Act, as its name implies, is designed to protect 'consumers'. Businesses can presumably look after themselves through contractual remedies and insurance.

However, 'consumer' is a slightly misleading term when compared to the meaning given to it by other legislation: a worker in the factory, or the driver of the company car, injured as a result of a defective product can claim under CPA 1987. Similarly if that worker or driver suffers *personal* property damage, e.g., to his clothing (but not to the company's overalls) he can claim for that even though it happens at work.

(c)   *Damage less than £275.*

(4)   No damages shall be awarded . . . in respect of any loss of or damage to any property if the amount which would fall to be so awarded . . . does not exceed £275.

This lower threshold applies only to property, not personal injury. It will exclude the vast number of minor incidents of personal property damage which could otherwise flood the courts. Claims for these losses can still be pursued in contract and negligence, but in many cases will be met by household and other private insurance.

The £275 minimum takes account of any reduction in damages through contributory negligence. So, if the actual damage caused was £400 but the victim was found to be 50% contributorily negligent, then damages which 'fall to be so awarded' amount to £200, i.e., below the threshold.

TIME-LIMITS FOR BRINGING AN ACTION

Anyone wishing to claim under the Act against any of the persons liable will lose his right to do so 10 years from when that person supplied the product. He must *commence* proceedings before the 10 years are up, though the proceedings may continue for several years after.

A further limitation is that he must commence proceedings within three years of becoming aware of the damage, the defect and the identity of the defendant, subject to the ultimate cut-off at 10 years. So if he is injured five years after the product was supplied he has until year eight; if nine years 11 months after the time of supply he has just one month left to start proceedings.

For latent damage the three-year period commences on the 'date of knowledge' of the plaintiff.[9]

The reason for the 10-year limit is to prevent the threat of legal action stretching out for an unlimited period. Many products, of course, are not expected to last 10 years. The definition of 'defect' takes account of perishable and consumable items and others suffering wear and tear as part of what 'persons generally are entitled to expect'. Provided the producer gives instructions, if appropriate, on the need to use within a period, servicing, renewal of parts etc., he will not be liable.

Implications for record retention

The implication for producers is that for up to 10 years they face the possibility of legal action. The burden of proof is on the victim, and the older the product gets the more difficult it will be to show that it was defective when originally supplied. But once the victim has made substantive allegations the producer will need to find evidence to refute them.

Retention periods for documents and records on any safety-related product or process which could be used in defending a case should therefore ideally be kept for this period (and longer if an action has already been commenced). Failure to do so could make the defence unnecessarily difficult:

● If a record showing what inspection was carried out on the product has been thrown away after three years, how can the manufacturer prove that the alleged defect did not exist when an action is brought five years later?

● If the defect in question is in an 'anonymous' component part which was multi-sourced, how can the producer trace it back to a particular supplier unless he has kept the purchase orders and stock control records for that period? Unless he can do this, he will not be able to share liability with co-producers. From the component manufacturer's point of view, how can he show he did not supply the defective one in question?

● If sales and delivery records are not kept, how can the supplier prove the date of supply for establishing:

   (i)   the product was supplied more than 10 years ago, or before 1 March 1988;

   (ii) the reference point for what 'persons generally are entitled to expect', i.e., it was supplied before the expectation rose;

   (iii) the reference point for 'the state of scientific and technical knowledge' to make use of the development risks defence (see pages 62–66), i.e., at that time the knowledge did not exist to discover the defect?

● If the design and process records are not kept, how can a manufacturer prove that he was using relevant knowledge for the purpose of the development risks defence? (see pages 62–66).

For many records the retention period will need to be even longer, because the time-limit starts when the product is *supplied*, not when designed or manufactured. Design and pre-production records should be kept throughout the production period plus 10 years from when production ceases to provide evidence to refute alleged design defects.

To a lesser extent the purchasing and manufacturing records will need longer retention to cover the gap between receiving the materials and component parts, manufacturing the product and actually releasing it from stock by way of 'supply'.

The practical difficulties of retaining mountains of paper, tapes or even microfilm mean that for many producers the remote chance of some future law suit does not justify the expense and effort of storage. However, many vital records are probably discarded by staff unaware of the implications, or because the policy has always been to retain only for a certain number of years. Six years may have been chosen, because actions in contract and tort generally expire after that period.[10]

Producers should therefore review their document retention policy in view of the product liability implications. This will be discussed further in chapter 9.

Time of supply

The time of supply is when a producer, own-brander or importer supplies the product to another (not necessarily the user). A component manufacturer's exposure period will therefore expire before that of the finished product manufacturer. This will mean that as the time periods expire there will be fewer defendants to join in the action, and eventually the last one in the chain will be the only one liable.

Holding stocks for long periods can therefore cause legal as well as storage problems.

Products supplied before March 1988

The Act is not retrospective, so products supplied before 1 March 1988 are not covered. This provision[11] specifically applies to time of supply by a *producer* in the strict sense, not own-branders or importers. So if a producer supplies an own-brander before 1 March 1988, and the latter supplies a customer after that date, the Act does not apply.

If a product is supplied by one producer to another producer before 1 March 1988, incorporated into the latter's product and supplied by him after that date, the first producer will escape liability under the Act, the second will be fully liable.

This anomaly will last until stocks of materials delivered before 1 March 1988 are cleared.

WHAT DEFENCES ARE AVAILABLE?

This chapter has already discussed several limitations on liability:

(a)   For things outside the scope of 'product'.

(b)   For non-dangerous faults.

(c)   For products supplied before March 1988.

(d)   For damage occurring 10 years after the time of supply.

(e)   For purely financial loss.

(f)   For damage to business property.

(g)   For property damage less than £275.

Remember also that the victim has the burden of proof, and that damages may be reduced by his contributory negligence.

Section 4(1) provides six further defences:

(a)   *Compliance with legal requirements:*

that the defect is attributable to compliance with any requirement imposed by or under any enactment or with any Community obligation.

The crucial factor here is that the producer was obliged to comply; he had no choice. He must show that the defect was the *inevitable* result of compliance. Thus if a regulation specifies that a certain additive *must* be used in a certain food process, then if that additive causes harm the producer has a defence. But how can such food be 'defective' in the first place if it meets the legal requirement? What more is it that 'persons generally are entitled to expect' by way of safety? The defence would only seem to apply in rare cases where the legal requirement is itself inadequate because it is misconceived or outdated, e.g., latest research reveals the danger but producers cannot legally incorporate the new ideas.

There must be a direct link between the regulatory standard and the defect. Thus if a regulation for children's nightwear specifies that it must be made of non-flammable material, but a garment causes dermatitis, then the producer could be liable *unless* the irritant was an inevitable result of the process of making the material non-flammable.

In fact most regulations impose *minimum* standards rather than absolutes: they state minimum strengths, maximum heats, permissible proportions of various constituents etc. The test then is not simply that the producer complies with that bare minimum, but *by how much he exceeds it.* That is determined by the test of what 'persons generally are entitled to expect'. So if a majority of manufacturers of a type of product provide a level of safety well above that demanded by the legal minimum, then this defence may not succeed.

The principle is well illustrated by an American case some years ago when a Federal regulation for motor vehicles required the vehicle to be turned upside down in a jig, suspended above the ground, to check for any fuel leakage. A particular model passed that test, but the manufacturer knew that in a real roll-over accident the filler cap, which was exposed, could be crushed and all the fuel spill out. Roll-over tests had proved this. No action was taken because, as the test reports spelt out, the regulation had been satisfied. Yet other models, both in that producer's range and from other manufacturers, had recessed filler caps. The technology clearly existed to make that model safer to a degree that consumers should be entitled to expect. When a claim for an accident involving a roll-over and subsequent fire was later brought, the manufacturer paid over $1 million in settlement.

Many standards (such as British Standards) followed by manufacturers are voluntary rather than mandatory. Compliance with such standards is arguably meeting the consumer expectation, but is not within this defence.

It is a common misconception that compliance with legal or other standards automatically exempts a producer from liability. It does not. It is a defence to a criminal charge for breaking safety requirements (see chapter 5), but not necessarily to a civil claim.

The consequences of this for design philosophy are discussed in chapter 6.

(b)   *The product was not supplied:*

that the person proceeded against did not at any time supply the product to another.

'Supply' is defined by s. 46, and includes:

(i)   Selling, hiring out or lending the goods.

(ii)   Entering into a hire-purchase agreement to furnish the goods.

(iii)   The performance of any contract for work and materials to furnish the goods.

(iv)   Providing the goods in exchange for any consideration (including trading stamps) other than money.

(v)   Providing the goods in or in connection with the performance of any statutory function.

(vi)   Giving the goods as a prize or gift.

Thus there does not have to be a sale for money: free promotional gifts incur the same liabilities as products sold for profit.

The defence will apply if the product is still within the manufacturer's premises (whether being manufactured, tested, stored or used), if it has been stolen or scrapped.

Prototypes being tested by the manufacturer would not be 'supplied' to another, but presumably would be if given to someone else to test.

Products such as tools and equipment made by the manufacturer for use inside his own factory or outside by his own employees would be covered by other legislation, such as the Factories Act 1961 and the Employer's Liability (Defective Equipment) Act 1969.

The defence seems extremely simple: 'I did not supply it, someone else did'. The defendant will have to prove, on the 'balance of probabilities' test used in civil cases, that he did not supply, leaving the victim or the other defendants to identify who did.

Two situations present problems:

(i)   Counterfeit products: normally the genuine producer has such an intimate knowledge of his product that he can point out the differences, but with increasing sophistication this becomes more difficult. Tactics have to be devised to beat the counterfeiters: hidden characteristics, code number systems, tiny markings etc.

(ii)   'Anonymous' products which could have come from other suppliers. The defendant will need to have records or other means of showing that the defective one in question was not supplied by him.

(c) *Not supplied by a business:*

(i)   that the only supply of the product to another by the person proceeded against was otherwise than in the course of a business of that person's; and

(ii)   that section 2(2) above does not apply to that person or applies to him by virtue only of things done otherwise than with a view to profit.

This excludes a sale or other supply by a private person of products manufactured by someone else. If the product is home-made, then liability could only arise if sold with a view to profit, e.g., making home-made jam to be given to the church fair would be excluded, selling it to tourists would not.

CPA 1987 is geared at making a business liable for defects, not a private individual. It is therefore similar to the Sale of Goods Act 1979 and the Supply of Goods and Services Act 1982 which, in respect of merchantable quality and fitness for purpose, impose liability only on those acting 'in the course of a business'. The combined effect of these Acts is that a private supplier can only be civilly liable for defects caused by his negligence or by breach of a specific safety regulation (for which there is the defence of exercising due diligence — see chapter 5). He will not face strict liability under CPA 1987, Part I.

(d)   *Not defective when supplied:*

that the defect did not exist in the product at the relevant time.

In practice this is the most important defence. The relevant time is when originally supplied (in the case of electricity this is defined as when generated, so defects caused by failures during distribution are not covered).

Many products have short life spans and will become dangerous if not used within that time. Others require service and renewal of parts to remain safe. Even durable products suffer wear and tear. Misuse, modification and deliberate tampering can occur. Warnings and instructions get lost or thrown away.

The producer (own-brander etc.) will not be liable if he can show that when he supplied the product there was no defect, i.e., it met the consumer expectation *at that time.* Where there are several producers, the relevant time is when each supplied on to the next.

This emphasises once again the need for record retention to have evidence to refute allegations. As well as the design and manufacturing records, the producer should also be able to prove what instructions, warnings, service schedules, recommendations, use-by dates etc. were issued. Records of owners, service history, usage and other details of the product's treatment may be worth keeping: the damage can then more easily be attributed to misuse, lack of service etc., rather than an original defect.

Malicious product tampering by terrorists, campaigners, extortionists and other disgruntled characters presents a major threat to consumer safety. If this tampering occurs *before* the time of supply, e.g., an employee deliberately sabotages the product before it leaves the factory, then the producer would be strictly liable because the product is defective. If it occurs *after* the time of supply by the producer (e.g., on retail premises) then he has a defence under s. 4, so will not face strict liability if someone suffers damage as a result (though the retailer might be liable for breach of s. 14 of the Sale of Goods Act 1979). Even though the producer may not be strictly liable in the latter case, this does not mean he can ignore the threat. If he has been warned by the perpetrators, or becomes aware of the danger, then failure to take all reasonable steps to eliminate it could be negligence and possibly criminal recklessness.

A further problem is that the producer's or retailer's insurance policy may exclude liability for such deliberate acts. The chances of recovering from the perpetrators, if they are caught, are in practice remote.[12]

(e)   *Development risks defence (sometimes referred to as the 'state of the art' defence):*

that the state of scientific and technical knowledge at the relevant time was not such that a producer of products of the same description as the product in question might be expected to have discovered the defect if it had existed in his products while they were under his control.

The defence would apply as follows: suppose a pharmaceutical company develops a new drug to combat a particular disease hitherto incurable. Extensive testing is carried out, using all available scientific and technological knowledge and following the best industry practices of the time. Years after it has been marketed a link is discovered between the drug and heart disease. This discovery is only made possible by new scientific methods developed in the meantime. The defect existed when the drug was put into circulation, but could not be detected at that time. The producer escapes liability.

This means that a victim can remain uncompensated for damage caused by defects. It goes against the spirit of strict liability for defective products, and has been the subject of fierce debate.

Consumers argue that if a producer puts into circulation a product which is later found to be defective, he should be made to compensate the victims, even though he could not be faulted on his research, development and manufacturing techniques. After all, the producer stands to make a profit, is probably well-insured and can afford to pay compensation. The cost can be spread by a small increase in the price over his product range. The individual victim cannot afford not to be compensated.

Producers counter that it is not fair that they should be accountable for defects they could not possibly detect; that technical innovation (particularly in the field of drugs) would be stunted without the defence; that insurance premiums would rocket in high-risk industries; that they would be put at a disadvantage with overseas producers in countries where fault is still a prerequisite of liability (such as Japan).

Arguments such as these were a major stumbling block in finding an acceptable formula for the Directive. Certain member States insisted on the inclusion of a development risks defence, some were totally opposed, others wanted it for certain categories of product only. The result is that the Directive provides for derogation. Around half the members have joined Britain in adopting a form of the defence.

A further complication is that Britain's version of the defence differs significantly from how it is stated in Article 7(e) of the Directive:

> that the state of scientific and technical knowledge at the time when he put the product into circulation was not such as to enable the existence of the defect to be discovered.

Thus the test in the Directive is whether the knowledge existed to discover the defect. It would not be satisfied if somewhere there existed such knowledge, no matter how difficult or expensive it might have been for the particular producer to apply it. So, if an aircraft manufacturer has the technology to test for internal imperfections in metal parts used in an aircraft's wings, then a bicycle manufacturer must use that same technology on the frames of his bicycles if the defence is to apply. In CPA 1987 the test is whether a producer of similar products might have been expected to have discovered the defect, so that one bicycle manufacturer will be compared with other bicycle manufacturers.

We await the first test cases, and meanwhile can only predict how the defence will be interpreted. Most commentators think it will very rarely apply in practice. It is really intended to protect those producers at the forefront of technology, where certain risks are justifiable for the overall benefit of progress. For the average manufacturer the failure to discover a defect is not due to a lack of scientific and technological knowledge in the industry, but a failure to apply such knowledge. This failure is not simply a matter of saving money. With volume production of such things as cars and washing machines, it is not feasible to apply latest technology immediately it is discovered: development, purchasing, retooling, training etc. can take years, and meanwhile production continues.

Let us take the example of a bicycle manufacturer. Suppose two parts of the metal frame are welded together and that this is the normal technique in the industry. There is a very slight risk that internal faults in the weld could eventually cause the frame to break and cause damage. Several possibilities arise:

(i)   The manufacturer does nothing, even though there is equipment available in the market and used by certain other bicycle manufacturers to test for faults. He would be strictly liable for damage.

(ii)   To test for such faults the manufacturer puts every frame through an X-ray machine, the very latest and best piece of detection equipment available. Unfortunately, that equipment cannot guarantee 100% detection: it is only 99% effective. One defective weld gets through the test and causes an accident. The manufacturer can use the defence.

(iii) A new version of that equipment becomes available, giving 99.5% effectiveness. The manufacturer decides that it is not worth buying for the marginal improvement in detection rate. Here another bicycle manufacturer might have discovered the defect, because he might have used the latest equipment.

No mention is made of the size of the producer: the fact that larger producers can afford the latest technology but small ones cannot is irrelevant — it is the nature of the product that counts, not the producer. The larger producers can therefore set the standard of expectation and effectively sabotage attempts by their smaller rivals to use the defence.

(iv)   What if all the world's bicycle manufacturers refused to buy the new equipment? By the wording of Article 7(e) of the Directive the defence would not apply, because the knowledge exists. Even under CPA 1987, s. 4(1)(e), it could still be argued that they might be expected to have used the knowledge. If the courts do interpret s. 4(1)(e) in this way, then a producer cannot assume that the traditional methods and standards of his industry will be a guaranteed defence.

(v)   The equipment can give 100% detection effectiveness, but is only used on a sample basis. Say 1 in 50 frames are subjected to the test, and if that one passes it is assumed that the previous (or next) 49 are safe, but with a remote statistical probability that some are not. By using the equipment the manufacturer admits the knowledge exists and might have detected the defect. So unless he does 100% testing, or his sample system makes it impossible for defects to get through, then presumably he could be liable.

(vi)   A metal frame of similar dimensions to that on a bicycle forms part of the structure of an aircraft. The consequences of a weld failure there, however remote, would be so catastrophic that the aircraft manufacturer devises some other method of joining, i.e., the knowledge exists to design and manufacture a metal frame without using susceptible welds at all. However, this is a very expensive method. Would the bicycle manufacturer be liable for failure to apply that method?

This is not a question of what knowledge is available to discover defects in welds, but whether the design should incorporate welds in the first place. This brings us back to the definition of 'defect', i.e., what 'persons generally are entitled to expect'. People expect bicycles to be of a reasonable price; the likelihood of failure is remote and the consequences not that serious compared to an aircraft crashing, so the huge cost of marginally improving the safety of the frame cannot be justified. Provided that other producers of similar bicycles use welds, then the design is not necessarily defective despite the fact that an ultimately safer, but vastly more expensive method is possible. So, by using welds *and* the scientific and technical knowledge expected of bicycle manufacturers to test for defects therein, the bicycle producer can escape liability. This is what is generally referred to as the 'state of the art'.

The expressions 'state of the art' and 'development risks' are sometimes used as shorthand for the s. 4(1)(e) defence. Neither precisely reflects what that defence provides. 'State of the art' is generally used to embrace two concepts adopted in CPA 1987 by, first, the notion of 'defect' in terms of expected safety features and, secondly, as a defence to liability where a defect is undiscoverable at the time. This second limb is what is referred to as 'development risks', but, as we have seen, the defence is not simply concerned with risks only discoverable by later scientific and technological developments.

The 'relevant time' for assessing the state of scientific and technical knowledge (and the meaning of 'defect') is the time of supply — not design or manufacture. If a producer has stocks of finished products awaiting dispatch, and the state of knowledge meanwhile changes to enable him to discover potential defects, then he would be expected to take appropriate action on those products.

(f)   *Defect in the subsequent product, not the component part*

that the defect —

(i)   constituted a defect in a product ('the subsequent product') in which the product in question had been comprised; and

(ii)   was wholly attributable to the design of the subsequent product or to compliance by the producer of the product in question with instructions given by the producer of the subsequent product.

A component or material producer has this opportunity to avoid the liability he would otherwise share on a joint or several basis with the producer using his component. For example, if a manufacturer buys a small bolt to hold together two heavy parts on his product, which then breaks, the bolt producer can say: 'Nothing wrong with my bolt — you overloaded it'; or: 'You specified this type of bolt, and that's what I supplied'.

To succeed on the first part of this defence, the component producer must show that there would have been no failure in his product if the subsequent product had been properly designed and manufactured. If the component partly contributed to the failure, then he will be liable (though he may manage to share that liability).

The component producer must, of course, provide appropriate instructions and warnings for non-obvious dangers and limitations (see chapter 6). If he knows of the intended usage and doubts the suitability of his component, he should communicate his reservations and keep a record of this.

To succeed on the second part he must show that the component which failed was made that way on the instructions of the subsequent producer. If he has had some involvement in design decisions, e.g., collaborative research and development, then the defence would not apply. If the subsequent producer has given specific instructions, then records should be kept together with any warnings or reservations expressed to him.

Producers of standard 'off-the-shelf' components should retain evidence that they were bought on that basis, without being informed of the special usages intended.

The subsequent producer will wish to prevent his component supplier escaping a share of any future liability. His tactics would be to involve the supplier in design and development, making clear the uses and stresses to which the component will be exposed, the intended manufacturing process, the proposed market, the after-sales support etc., then give the supplier the opportunity to test the finished product to verify the component's suitability. He should obtain and retain the supplier's written concurrence at the various stages (the 'sign-offs'). The terms of purchase should state that the supplier is aware of and accepts responsibility for the intended uses.

While such involvement and concurrence is common practice during the design phase of a product, problems often arise later. Shortages occur, so either the supplier substitutes an alternative component or the subsequent producer uses something else that appears suitable. One of them makes a minor change to his product which he wrongly assumes will not affect the integrity of the other's, so there is no communication of that change.

These defences provide some protection for a producer. While the CPA 1987 establishes a strict liability system, it does not impose absolute liability.

CHOICE OF JURISDICTION: FORUM SHOPPING

Many product liability cases will involve victims and defendants from more than one country. The product itself may have been assembled in one country from imported components. It may have been exported and sold in another country, but then taken somewhere else where the accident occurred. Where does the victim bring his case and against whom?

Often he will have a choice, and will then opt for the jurisdiction which he perceives as offering the most advantageous outcome. The factors include not just which law offers the best chance of winning, but a range of practical aspects:

(a) The level of damages.

(b)   Legal costs: how much and who pays, win or lose?

(c)   Availability of legal aid.

(d)   The delay before the case is heard.

(e)   Likelihood and delay of an appeal.

(f)   The rules on admissibility of evidence, discovery of documents and other disclosures.

(g)   Availability of witnesses, experts, medical opinions.

(h)   The quality of the judges, juries (if used) and the general legal system.

(i)   Other victims who might become part of a class action (if permitted) or otherwise help pool resources.

He may also have a choice over whom to sue, and will then be influenced by:

(a)   Can he sue on a joint or several basis?

(b)   Does the defendant have a 'deep pocket', i.e., adequate resources and/or insurance?

(c)   Can the defendant go into bankruptcy or liquidation to avoid paying?

(d)   Is insurance compulsory?

Within the European Community one might assume that the move towards harmonisation would remove any advantage of bringing a case in one member State rather than another. Not so. The result of derogations permitted by the Directive, together with other variations in the laws and procedures of member States can make a significant difference. The Directive also does not affect the rights of victims under existing national laws, e.g., contract and negligence. These differ, and may offer better alternative routes.

There are three permitted derogations:

(a)   Inclusion of primary agricultural produce and game. To date there is uniformity: no member State has indicated its intention to include these as 'products'.

(b) A financial ceiling on damage payable for death or injury caused by the same defect of 70 million ECU (the European currency unit) which is about £40 million. Britain has not adopted this limit, nor have the majority of States who have so far drafted legislation. Germany and Greece are among those who have it.

(c) The 'development risks' defence. This is by far the most important derogation, with Members roughly evenly split. France, Belgium Greece and Luxembourg are among those who will not permit such a defence at all. Germany will not allow it in respect of death or injury from pharmaceuticals. Britain, Ireland, the Netherlands, Denmark and probably Italy intend to apply it to all products. The position will be reviewed in 1995 when the EC Commission reports on the operation of the derogations to the Council of Ministers, who will then try to achieve harmony.

So, within the EC a victim faced with a claim where the 'development risk' defence might be raised (e.g., injury caused by an allegedly defective drug) would prefer not to bring the case in Britain. He would stand a better chance in Germany, where that defence does not apply to drugs. However, Germany has included the financial ceiling, so if there are many other victims of the same defect raising the possible damages above that level, then France or Belgium would be an even better choice.

The rules for determining whether a plaintiff has a choice of forum are laid down by the Convention on Jurisdiction and Enforcement of Judgments in Civil and Commercial Matters (the Brussels Convention). In combination with the Directive, which for most manufactured goods provides that there is more than one person treated as 'producer', several possibilities arise.

Let us take an example: suppose a German component manufacturer supplies an English company with parts for assembling into a finished product, which is then sold to a French distributor. A Dutchman on holiday in France buys the product, takes it home and later suffers an injury, allegedly due to a defect in the German component.

Who can he sue?

(a) Under the Directive, the German and English producers, either jointly or severally.

(b) The French distributor:

(i)   under the Directive if the distributor cannot identify the producer;

(ii)   under French laws of contract and tort applicable to sellers of goods.

Where can he sue?

The Convention provides various options:

(a)   A defendant can be sued in his 'place of domicile', i.e., the English producer can be sued in an English court, the French distributor in France.

(b)   If there is more than one defendant, all of them may be sued in the courts of the State where any *one* of them is domiciled, e.g., the German producer in an English court.

(c)   He can sue in 'the place where the harmful event occurred', i.e., in Holland where the injury occurred.

The court presented with the case interprets the meaning of 'place of domicile' and 'place where the harmful event occurred' according to its national rules. So, one State might say the harmful event occurred when and where the product was sold, another where the injury was sustained. Under UK legislation 'domicile' is deemed if the defendant has resided in the UK for the last three months before the proceedings started. A company has a domicile in the place of its 'seat': in the UK this means its registered office or where central management control is exercised.

A victim within the EC of a defective product made outside the EC will always be able to bring a case under the Directive and Convention because there will be an importer treated as producer. If the victim cannot identify the importer, then the supplier becomes liable unless he can so identify.

Victims outside the EC trying to sue EC producers will have to look to their national rules and conventions to establish whether they can bring those producers into their own jurisdiction.

Implications for producers and other defendants

Where products are likely to circulate throughout the EC, then all producers, own-branders, EC importers or distributors unable to identify producers should assume they will be exposed to product liability claims in any member State.

A component supplier may not even be aware of the destination of the final product, yet faces possible liability under less favourable laws than either in his own domicile or in that of the finished product manufacturer. The 'development risk' defence may therefore prove ineffective when a victim uses the Convention rules to bring his case in a State which has not adopted that defence.

Insurance cover will, in practice, have to be taken on the basis of no 'development risk' defence and no financial ceiling on damages. So these two derogations are of little practical relevance for such products.

The problems of cost and availability of insurance make it essential to have appropriate contractual arrangements to share liability, e.g., the EC importer ensuring he can get a full indemnity from the overseas manufacturer for any liabilities and costs incurred, including recalls and loss of profit.

SUMMARY

Implementation of the Directive establishes the principle of strict liability for defective products throughout the EC. A victim no longer has to show that the producer was negligent, or be party to a contract.

The wide definition of 'producer' and extension of liability to others in the distribution chain mean that a victim has an easily identifiable target. The principle of joint and several liability means that if one defendant cannot pay, another will.

While liability is strict, it is not absolute. There are a number of defences and provisos to enable a defendant to escape all or part of liability. However, apart from these it is not possible to exclude liability to victims by means of exclusion clauses.

Unlimited damages are payable in most member States.

Producers and distributors of products circulating in the EC should assume they will be subject to the laws of any member State, and not rely on the more favourable laws of their own country.

Producers should be aware of the increased legal exposure and can take steps to minimise it. This is the subject of later chapters in this book.

NOTES

1 The Council of the European Communities Directive of 25 July 1985 (85/374/EEC) on the approximation of the laws, regulations and administrative provisions of the member States concerning liability for defective products.

2 DTI explanatory note, 'Implementation of EC Directive on Product Liability', November 1985. This was also the opinion during passage of the Bill through Parliament.

3 Civil Liability (Contribution) Act 1978.

4 Subject to the Unfair Contract Terms Act 1977. See chapter 2.

5 In *Photo Production Ltd* v *Securicor Transport Ltd* [1980] AC 827 at p. 843.

6 CPA 1987, s. 4(2). The electricity industry is subject to various duties to maintain supplies imposed by other statutes and regulations.

7 See R. Kidner 'Toxic waste and strict liability for products' (1988) 138 NLJ 379.

8 For example, for nuisance or under the rule in *Rylands* v *Fletcher*, see chapter 4. There are various statutory controls on the disposal of waste, e.g., the Control of Pollution Act 1974.

9 Limitation Act 1980, as amended by CPA 1987, sch 1.

10 Limitation Act 1980.

11 CPA 1987, s. 50(7).

12 The tamperer could be sued by the producer or retailer for the tort of trespass to goods, or a criminal court could make a compensation order under the s. 35 of the Powers of Criminal Courts Act 1973, as amended by the Criminal Justice Act 1982, s. 67. This assumes the tamperer has the means to pay!

4

Civil Liability Under Other Torts

The majority of civil claims in respect of damage caused by allegedly defective products will be based on breach of contract or Part I of the Consumer Protection Act 1987. However, in both these areas there are limitations, exceptions and defences, so there will be circumstances where a victim has to pursue a claim through some other legal route.

Four particular torts are relevant to product liability:

(a) Negligence.

(b) Breach of statutory duty.

(c) Nuisance.

(d) Liability under the rule in *Rylands* v *Fletcher*.

NEGLIGENCE

Negligence means breach of a duty to take *reasonable care*, resulting in loss or injury. Until 1988 it was the main basis for an action by a third-party victim against a producer.

The modern law of negligence was established in the famous case of the snail in the bottle of ginger-beer — *Donoghue* v *Stevenson*.[1] The plaintiff went to a café with her friend who bought for her a bottle of Stevenson's ginger-beer, which came in a dark opaque bottle. She drank some of it, poured out the rest, and then discovered the decomposed remains of a snail (undoubtedly the most famous dead snail in legal history!). She suffered severe gastro-enteritis. Clearly the beer was unmerchantable and unfit for drinking, but she had no contract on which to sue the retailer. Instead she sued the manufacturer, who was held to have broken a duty of care.

The case established the general principle stated in the following way by Lord Atkin:

> You must take reasonable care to avoid acts or omissions which you can reasonably foresee would be likely to injure your neighbour. Who, then, in law is my neighbour? The answer seems to be — persons who are so closely and directly affected by my act that I ought reasonably to have them in contemplation as being so affected when I am directing my mind to the acts or omissions which are called in question.

Applying this to a manufacturer:

> ... a manufacturer of products, which he sells in such a form as to show that he intends them to reach the ultimate consumer in the form in which they left him with no reasonable possibility of intermediate examination, and with the knowledge that the absence of reasonable care in the preparation or putting up the products will result in an injury to the consumer's life or property, *owes a duty to the consumer to take that reasonable care.*

Problem for the victim: how can he prove that the manufacturer failed to take 'reasonable care'? Unless he can do this, no damages are payable.

Since the principle was first established it has been extended to cover many other possible defendants: designers, installers, assemblers, packers, retailers, repairers, servicers and anyone else connected with the product who in some way can be said to have owed a duty of care to the plaintiff, who failed to take reasonable care as a result of which (in full or in part) the plaintiff suffered loss or injury.

The negligence can relate not just to the design and manufacture of the product itself, but to aspects such as packaging, marketing, warnings and instructions, advice, after-sale service etc.

Liability is limited to injury and physical damage. Following a number of recent cases[2] it now seems settled that it does not extend to purely economic loss. In this respect it is similar to CPA 1987. Such economic losses are claimable in contract.

Negligence and strict liability

Negligence is 'fault-based' as opposed to the 'no-fault' or 'strict liability' concept in contract and under CPA 1987.

This crucial difference is illustrated by the 1938 case of *Daniels v R. White & Sons Ltd*.[3] Mr Daniels went to a public house and bought from the licensee, Mrs Tarbard, a jug of beer and a bottle of R. White's lemonade. He took this lemonade home, mixed some with the beer, and both he and his wife drank it. They both suffered an intense burning sensation and at once thought they had been poisoned. On analysis it was discovered that the lemonade contained 38 grains (about 2.5 g) of carbolic acid.

Mr Daniels sued Mrs Tarbard as seller under what is now s. 14(2) of the Sale of Goods Act 1979. Mrs Daniels could not do so, because she was not a buyer.

The product was clearly unmerchantable, for which the seller was strictly liable, i.e., without having to establish any lack of care. Even though she could not be expected to remove the paper seal over the bottle stopper and chemically analyse the contents, she was liable.

Both Mr and Mrs Daniels sued R. White & Sons Ltd in negligence, and failed. R. White & Sons Ltd showed that it had an excellent system of bottling, which it considered 'foolproof', that it had produced thousands of bottles without complaint, and had exercised all reasonable care.

So, for the same defect causing the same sort of injury, Mr Daniels obtained compensation from the morally blameless Mrs Tarbard; Mrs Daniels obtained no compensation through inability to prove negligence.

The actual decision has since been questioned, and if the same facts occurred today a court would probably find that the mere presence of 2.5 g of carbolic acid must show that the manufacturer was negligent.[4]

The standard of 'reasonable care' expected by the courts has also considerably increased since 1938.[5]

But the principle remains, as shown by some of the drug tragedies, where manufacturers have put harmful products into circulation and escaped liability.

Mrs (and Mr) Daniels could have claimed negligence by Mrs Tarbard, but did she fail to take reasonable care? As a retailer her duty was first to take care in selecting a supplier, and in the absence of any suspicion that the lemonade produced by R. White & Sons Ltd had a history of defects she could not be expected to do more than choose an apparently safe brand. Secondly she had a duty to carry out reasonable checks on the product, which here can be no more than a cursory visual examination. She could not be expected to undertake a chemical analysis, or indeed take a swig from each bottle to check the taste! Thirdly she had a duty to pass on any necessary warnings and instructions for use (not relevant here) and finally to take remedial action if it became clear that the goods were defective (e.g., withdrawing stocks from the shelves).

In many cases the simple fact that the product is defective is sufficient to prove that someone was negligent, and the plaintiff does not have to point his finger at the *exact* place where the fault occurred.[6] But he does have to build up sufficient evidence to show, on a balance of probabilities, that the defendant was responsible. So, in *Evans v Triplex Safety Glass Co. Ltd,*[7] where a car windscreen suddenly shattered and injured the occupants, the claim against the windscreen manufacturer failed because the defect could have been caused by the car manufacturer straining the glass during fitting into its frame. Furthermore, the car was a year old so the defect might not have existed at the time of manufacture, but could have been due to some intervening factor.

With a complex product like a motor vehicle several manufacturers and distributors may be involved. Suppose the brakes on a new car are defective, causing a crash. The fault is found to be a defective valve in the brake master cylinder. That valve was made by a specialist valve manufacturer who supplied it to a brake cylinder manufacturer, who supplied the complete cylinder unit to the car manufacturer. The finished car goes to an area distributor and then on to a dealer for sale to the customer.

When the victims of the crash sue in negligence, each of the possible defendants can try to pass the buck. The dealer might say: 'We did everything we could by following the pre-delivery inspection procedure, which did not reveal any defect'.

The area distributor: 'We are not responsible for inspecting brakes. The car seemed OK when we handled it.'

The car manufacturer: 'We buy in brake cylinders as complete sealed units. We could not see the internal defect on this one. We carry out rigorous checks on our suppliers, dismantle a sample of each batch, and check the operation of all brakes at the end of the line. This defect got through despite our excellent quality control systems. It was a one-in-a-million freak. We will try to ensure it does not happen again. If you want to blame anyone, blame the component manufacturers.'

Similarly the cylinder manufacturer: 'We buy valves from a reputable manufacturer, who has excellent quality control. We do tests and checks, but cannot reasonably be expected to dismantle every valve. Blame the valve manufacturer.'

So finally the valve manufacturer has to put up a defence, which is going to be difficult but not impossible: 'We have excellent quality control systems. This has never happened before. No other valve manufacturer would have detected such a defect.'

Maybe the car manufacturer could be accused of negligent design by not having a back-up or fail-safe mechanism, but that could be defended by showing that such sophistication is not generally adopted by car makers. Provided the car has the *expected* technology (a handbrake, low-fluid warning light, dual-circuit brakes), and despite these the crash still occurs, then the fact that it does not have *every conceivable* safety device will not necessarily mean it was negligently designed.

Negligence does not mean failure to take every possible care, only reasonable care in the circumstances.

So, if anyone, it will probably be the valve manufacturer who is liable in negligence and will have to pay damages. But what if he has meanwhile gone out of business, or lacks the resources or insurance cover for such a large claim? No one else in the chain has been found negligent, so the victims lose out.

The burden of proof in negligence cases is on the plaintiff, and this may involve a long and costly legal battle. Often it is an individual up against a large company with the resources to mount a vigorous defence, particularly since its reputation is on the line. It is not simply concerned with paying out one lot of damages, but with the long term effects on its sales, the possibility of other victims jumping on the band-wagon, recalls, redesign, increased insurance premiums etc. This resistance to admit negligence, even where the facts point clearly to it, may cause the plaintiff to drop the case or accept a small pre-trial settlement.

Pressure for reform of this unsatisfactory situation eventually resulted in the Consumer Protection Act 1987, Part I. This now makes proof of negligence unnecessary in respect of 'defective products'. Its other great advantage for the victim is the range of potential defendants, with joint and several liability, so more than one of the manufacturers or distributors may be liable and have a 'deep pocket' from which to pay.

So what is the relevance of negligence today?

Despite the wide coverage of Part I of the CPA 1987, there are circumstances where it will not apply. Remember also that contractual claims are limited by the privity rule.

Part I of CPA 1987 casts a wide net over categories of person who can be liable, but there may be others who are responsible for a defect, before or after it is produced, who are not covered. For example, if the manufacturer used an independent designer, consultant or other expert, and that design is defective, then the manufacturer is strictly liable as producer. The designer is not a producer. If that manufacturer goes into liquidation or is unable to pay for the damage, then the victim's claim against the designer would depend on proof of negligence.

Similarly a carrier, warehouser, distributor or retailer might have damaged the product, rendering it defective, but would not be strictly liable as a producer (provided he can identify the producer). Here the actual producer could escape liability by showing that at the time of supply by him the product was not defective.

Part I has other limitations:

(a)   It does not apply to all products (primary agricultural produce is excepted).

(b)   It does not cover damage to business property.

(c)   It does not cover damage to personal property below £275.

(d)   The product has to be 'supplied'.

(e)   The supply must be by a business or for profit.

(f)   The defect must exist at the time of supply, so failure to rectify defects occurring later is not covered.

(g)   It is not retrospective: products supplied before 1 March 1988 are not covered.

For cases brought in the USA, proof of negligence may lead to an award of punitive damages, i.e., huge amounts in addition to normal compensation.

Thus despite the enormous significance of CPA 1987, there are still situations where liability depends on negligence.

Who does the victim sue for negligence: the company or the individual employee responsible?

The principle of *vicarious liability* makes an employer liable for the acts and omissions of employees during the course of their employment (but not for their crimes, see chapter 5). In theory the victim could sue the employee personally, but there is no point:

(a) He would have to identify that employee.

(b) The employee is not worth suing and probably has no insurance cover.

(c) The employer has more resources and usually insurance cover.

The employer (or more likely his insurance company) having paid out damages could claim an indemnity from the employee. Again this is highly unlikely:

(a) It would be bad for industrial relations.

(b) The employee does not have the resources.

(c) If the employee does have insurance cover, then one insurance company would be claiming from another, not from the employee.

So in practice the employee does not pay the victim directly or indirectly for his negligence. He may be disciplined or in certain cases dismissed for breach of his contract of employment. His promotion chances will no doubt suffer!

Avoiding liability for negligence

The simple way to avoid liability is not to be negligent! But what does this mean? How much care is 'reasonable'? Various factors have to be taken into account in achieving a realistic balance:

(a) The foreseeability of injury or damage occurring.

(b)   The likely extent of such injury.

(c)   The obviousness of the danger to the person at risk.

(d)   The utility of the product as it is compared to the diminished utility by a change in design.

(e)   The cost and practicality of eliminating the risk.

Hundreds of cases have been brought to the courts to test these factors. Standards change, and new factors emerge. Recent cases suggest a very high level of care.[8]

The defendant (designer, manufacturer etc.) must therefore be able to show that he has tried to foresee the risks associated with his product, by testing, observation, reaction to failures etc., including foreseeable misuse; that he has considered alternative designs and methods, made comparisons with techniques used by others dealing with similar products; that he is aware of developments in technology which could improve safety. Above all he must show that he is exercising the same level of care as might be expected of anyone else in a similar position. If all the manufacturers of a particular type of product adopt the same safety levels, then any victim will have difficulty establishing negligence (assuming that all mandatory requirements have been met), though the 'trade norm' is not a guaranteed defence. It is when one manufacturer falls below the norm that the exposure dramatically increases (see chapter 6).

Contributory negligence by the victim

The defendant may not be entirely responsible for the damage. If the victim is partly to blame, for example, by continuing to use a product which he knows is defective, then the damages are reduced proportionately. The Law Reform (Contributory Negligence) Act 1945, s. 1 provides:

> Where any person suffers damage as the result partly of his own fault and partly of the fault of any other person or persons, a claim in respect of that damage shall not be defeated by reason of the fault of the person suffering the damage, but the damages recoverable in respect thereof shall be reduced to such extent as the court thinks just and equitable having regard to the claimant's share in the responsibility for the damage.

Assumption of the risk by the victim

Another possible defence for the producer is that the victim voluntarily assumed the risk. The principle is, *volenti non fit iniuria* — 'to him who is willing no harm is done'. This has mainly been applied to spectators and participants in sporting events who have been injured by flying balls, hard tackles etc. For the defence to operate there must be more than just awareness of a risk: the plaintiff must freely assent to it in full knowledge of the physical dangers *and* of the legal risk, i.e., the risk of actual damage for which there will be no redress at law.[9]

Thus, anyone using an electric saw assumes the normal risks associated with it, such as chopping his finger off (assuming the saw incorporated appropriate guards and warnings). But he does not assume the risk of being electrocuted by a defect in the saw.

These two defences are particularly useful to a manufacturer where the victim continued to use a product knowing it to be defective, or has failed to heed warnings and instructions. They apply both to negligence and strict liability under CPA 1987.

Shared liability with other defendants

Where two or more parties share in the blame, then the principle of joint and several liability applicable to contract and tort means that each defendant can be made fully liable. That does not mean the victim can get twice as much damages! It means he can sue them on a joint basis, or individually. If he chooses to sue just one defendant who pays out the damages, then that defendant can claim a contribution from the others. The Civil Liability (Contribution) Act 1978 operates to enable a just and equitable proportion to be recovered.

BREACH OF STATUTORY DUTY

Various statutes and regulations impose duties regarding the safety of products which if broken give rise to *criminal* offences e.g., the Food Act 1984, Health and Safety at Work etc. Act 1974, Electric Blankets (Safety) Regulations 1971 (SI 1971/1961). Breach of these can result in fines or other sanctions (see chapter 5). They are not *primarily* intended to give rise to civil claims for damages. However, there may be a civil claim in certain circumstances, known as 'breach of statutory duty'.

Contrary to popular belief, breach of a statute which creates criminal offences does not automatically give rise to a civil claim for damages by persons suffering loss or damage as a result of that breach.

Some statutes make it clear that they create only criminal offences. Others specifically provide that a civil claim can be brought, but the somewhat ridiculous position exists that many of them simply do not mention whether breach gives rise to a civil claim, leaving it to the courts to try to read into the statute the intention of Parliament who created it.

These 'criminal only' statutes do not necessarily deprive the victims of compensation. The criminal courts have discretionary power[10] to make compensation orders for personal injury, loss or damage for which a person has been convicted, but there are financial limits (£2,000 in a magistrates' court, unlimited in a Crown Court) and the power is not exercised on a regular basis.[11]

This confusing position is made more sensible by the Consumer Protection Act 1987. Part II of the Act (considered in chapter 5) gives the Secretary of State wide powers to make safety regulations in respect of particular goods. Around 40 such regulations passed under earlier legislation are now incorporated into this, covering a wide range of potentially hazardous consumer products. Breach of these regulations is an offence, punishable by fine and/or imprisonment, but s. 41(1) *specifically* provides that a civil claim can be brought by any person affected.

So, the producer of a product which is in breach of a safety regulation under Part II can be liable to pay a fine to the State up to the maximum level specified (generally £2,000) for the offence plus unlimited damages to the victim for breach of statutory duty. Safety regulations are, however, concerned solely with risks to personal safety, so damage to property is not within their scope.

Such a product will also invariably be considered as 'defective'under Part I, 'unmerchantable' under the Sale of Goods Act 1979, and possibly caused by negligence. So how does breach of statutory duty give a victim any advantage over these other routes to obtaining compensation? In two ways:

(a)   He may be spared the necessity of bringing a separate legal action if a successful criminal prosecution has been brought. Hopefully the criminal court will have awarded adequate compensation. If not, then the threat of a civil action will probably result in the offer by the defendant of an acceptable settlement because there can be no doubt about the outcome of the case.

       The evidence for a prosecution will be gathered by the enforcement authorities at public expense, saving the victim time and effort. If the prosecution fails, the victim may decide not to waste his time on a separate civil claim because the available evidence is unconvincing.

(b) It may give him someone else to sue, which will be important if the producer and other persons liable under CPA 1987, Part I (own-branders etc.), have gone out of business or cannot pay in full. Safety regulations generally apply to *any person* supplying the relevant goods, so retailers and others in the distribution chain can be liable for breach as well as producers.

Other statutes have a similar effect in extending the number of potential defendants. *Employers* face considerable liabilities under statute for the safety of equipment and premises. The Employer's Liability (Defective Equipment) Act 1969 imposes strict liability on an employer who supplies defective equipment which causes injury to an employee, where the defect is attributable wholly or partly to the fault of a third party (e.g., manufacturer, installer, repairer). Thus the employee has a right to sue the employer, without proof of negligence by the employer. He could also sue the equipment manufacturer (or anyone else responsible) in negligence or under CPA 1987, but normally there is no point. The Employers' Liability (Compulsory Insurance) Act 1969 requires all employers carrying on business in Great Britain (with certain exemptions[12]) to obtain insurance cover of £2 million against claims by one or more employees arising from any one occurrence. Having paid out, the employer (or his insurers) could seek an indemnity from the manufacturer or supplier responsible for the defect by claiming breach of contract.

The Factories Act 1961 and associated legislation makes *occupiers* of factories and other industrial and commercial premises responsible for the fencing of machinery, safety of lifts, cleanliness of gangways and a host of other potential hazards in the workplace. Some provisions mention 'reasonable' or 'all practical' steps to be taken, but others are strict.[13]

Again the employer or occupier who has paid out damages can seek indemnities from suppliers.

NUISANCE

The tort of private nuisance involves an unlawful interference with a person's use or enjoyment of land, or some right over or in connection with it,[14] e.g., noise, vibration, emissions of smells, dust, chemicals. Liability rests with the person causing the nuisance, usually from adjoining land. Public nuisance is more serious, and can be a criminal offence, involving interference with the comfort and convenience of a class of citizens.

To be 'unlawful' in practice means unreasonable, so certain annoying interferences have to be tolerated as a normal consequence of living in a particular area.[15] A plaintiff cannot take advantage of a peculiar sensitivity (e.g., keen sense of smell; allergy) if an ordinary person would not have been disturbed.[16]

Liability is not dependent on fault, as in negligence, so if an activity cannot by any care and skill be prevented from causing harm, then it cannot lawfully be undertaken at all unless authorised by statute or with the consent of all those affected by it. The harm is restricted to interfering with someone else's enjoyment or causing damage to property. Liability does not appear to extend to personal injury.[17]

Nuisance is not generally considered as a branch of product liability law. However, there are situations where the law of nuisance could fill a gap in the liability created by CPA 1987, providing a victim with a remedy without having to prove negligence or breach of contract. In relation to products, a nuisance could occur:

(a)   during the course of their manufacture (e.g. noise or emissions from the factory); or

(b)   by the person using the product (a noisy machine).

Neither of these situations is covered by CPA 1987.

Situation (a) is not covered because there has been no 'supply' of a product to another person.[18] So, someone living next door to the factory who suffers loss of enjoyment or damage to his property would be able to sue the occupier of the factory (i.e., the producer) for nuisance. The occupier might be liable in negligence and face criminal liability under the Health and Safety at Work etc. Act 1974 (see chapter 5), but both of these depend on a failure to exercise reasonable care, whereas nuisance does not.

Situation (b) is not covered because damage caused by nuisance is the responsibility of the person using the product, not the person who produced it. The law of nuisance therefore extends liability for defective products to *users* as well as producers.

THE RULE IN *RYLANDS* v *FLETCHER*[19]

This rule is basically a development of nuisance. The rule is that the person who, for his own purposes, brings on to his lands and collects and keeps there anything likely to do mischief if it escapes, must keep it at his peril, and, if he does not do so, is prima facie answerable for all the damage which is the natural consequence of its escape.

It is therefore concerned with *escapes*, and has been confined to non-natural use of land. So water lying on land after a heavy storm and flooding over neighbouring land is not covered, but water stored in a purpose-built reservoir would be if it leaked out. It has been applied to escapes of gas, oil, chemicals, toxic waste and electricity. Disasters such as Flixborough and Bhopal are potentially within the rule.

The rule imposes strict liability, so a plaintiff need not prove negligence or unreasonable use of land. However, it has several provisos and defences:

(a) There must be an escape *from* the defendant's land, so it does not apply where some dangerous substance leaks *within* the land (e.g., in the factory during manufacture) and causes damage.[20]

(b) The plaintiff may consent to the usage, expressly or impliedly (e.g., an occupier in a multi-storey building is deemed to have consented to the normal supply of gas, water etc. to the other occupants, so cannot use the rule when an escape damages him[21]).

(c) The source of the danger might be of 'common benefit' to the plaintiff (e.g., a fire sprinkler system throughout a building, where water floods into the plaintiff's premises on a lower floor[22])

(d) If the escape is due to the unauthorised act of a stranger (e.g., a trespasser or saboteur releasing the danger) then the owner of the land from which the material escaped is not liable.

(e) Some public bodies, such as gas and electricity boards, are exempted from liability by statute, provided they have taken reasonable care.

(f) If all else fails, the defendant can plead Act of God.[23]

The rule in *Rylands* v *Fletcher*, like nuisance, imposes strict liability on a *user*, not necessarily a producer or distributor. It therefore goes beyond liability in contract, negligence, or under CPA 1987.

SUMMARY

There will be situations where victims of defective products cannot bring a claim either in contract or under Part I of the CPA 1987. However, there are other legal routes, in particular, the law of negligence, which can provide a remedy. None of these have been abolished by implementation of CPA 1987: they continue as an alternative or additional basis of claim.

NOTES

1   *Donoghue* v *Stevenson* [1932] AC 562.

2   *Simaan General Contracting Co.* v *Pilkington Glass Ltd (No. 2)* [1988] QB 758;
Greater Nottingham Co-operative Society Ltd v *Cementation Piling & Foundations
Ltd* [1989] QB 71; *D & F Estates Ltd* v *Church Commissioners for England* [1988] 3
WLR 368.

3   *Daniels* v *R. White & Sons Ltd* [1938] 4 All ER 258.

4   The doctrine of *res ipsa loquitur* — 'the thing speaks for itself' — might be
invoked on similar facts. This means that 'a plaintiff prima facie establishes
negligence where: (i) it is not possible for him to prove precisely what was the
relevant act or omission which set in train the events leading to the accident; but
(ii) on the evidence as it stands at the relevant time it is more likely than not that
the effective cause of the accident was some act or omission of the defendant or
of someone for whom the defendant is responsible, which act or omission
constitutes a failure to take proper care' (per Megaw LJ in *Lloyde* v *West
Midlands Gas Board* [1971] 1 WLR 749 at p. 755). The doctrine effectively
switches the burden of proof on to the defendant to disprove negligence. It is
not often applied by the courts.

5   See for example *Hill* v *James Crowe (Cases) Ltd* [1978] ICR 298; *Winward* v
TVR Engineering Ltd [1986] BTLC 366.

6   See *Grant* v *Australian Knitting Mills Ltd* [1936] AC 85 for a case with similar
facts to *Daniels* v *R. White & Sons Ltd* [1983] 4 All ER 258 where the
manufacturer was found negligent.

7   [1936] 1 All ER 283.

8   For a full treatment of this subject see the standard texts on the law of tort,
e.g., *Winfield and Jolowicz on Tort*, 12th ed. by W.V.H. Rogers (London: Sweet &
Maxwell, 1984); *Salmond & Heuston on the Law of Torts*, 19th ed. by R.F.V.
Heuston and R.A. Buckley (London: Sweet & Maxwell, 1987); M. Brazier, *The
Law of Torts*, 8th ed. (London: Butterworths, 1988); *Clerk & Lindsell on Torts*,
14th ed. by R.W.M. Dias (London: Sweet & Maxwell, 1982).

9   *Bowater* v *Rowley Regis Corporation* [1944] KB 476; *Imperial Chemical
Industries Ltd* v *Shatwell* [1965] AC 656.

10   Powers of Criminal Courts Act 1973, s. 35 amended by Criminal Justice Act 1982, s. 67.

11   See P.S. Atiyah, 'Compensation orders and civil liability' [1979] Crim LR 504.

12   The main exemptions are for local authorities, statutory corporations and nationalised industries, who presumably can afford to pay. Minor exemptions are provided by the Employers' Liability (Compulsory Insurance) Exemption Regulations 1971 (SI 1971/1933).

13   See *Redgrave's Health and Safety in Factories,'* 2nd. ed. by I. Fife and E.A. Machin (London: Butterworths, 1982) for a full guide. Also M. Whincup, *Modern Employment Law*, 3rd ed. (London: Heinemann, 1980) for an excellent practical explanation.

14   Per Scott LJ in *Read v J. Lyons & Co. Ltd* [1947] AC 156.

15   *St Helens Smelting Co.* v *Tipping* (1865) 11 HL Cas 642.

16   *Robinson v Kilvert* (1889) 41 ChD 88.

17   See *Salmond and Heuston on the Law of Torts* (see note 8), ch. 4.

18   CPA 1987, ss. 4(1)(b) and 46.

19   (1868) LR 3 HL 330.

20   *Read v J. Lyons & Co. Ltd* [1945] KB 216; affirmed [1947] AC 156.

21   *Attorney-General* v *Cory Brothers & Co. Ltd* [1921] 1 AC 521.

22   *Peters v Prince of Wales Theatre (Birmingham) Ltd* [1943] KB 73.

23   *Nichols v Marsland* (1876) 2 ExD 1; *Greenock Corporation* v *Caledonian Railway Co.* [1917] AC 556.

5

Criminal Liability

The term 'product liability' is generally taken as referring to the *civil* liability of producers and suppliers to *compensate* victims of defective products. 'Product safety' or 'consumer safety' usually refers to *criminal* liabilities in respect of defective products. Safety legislation creating criminal offences aims primarily at *preventing* unsafe products causing damage by laying down standards and requirements, and by *punishing* or taking other measures against those who fail to meet them. Thus a producer can be criminally liable without any damage having occurred.

Until recently such safety legislation has been piecemeal: numerous separate regulations for specific products, e.g., food, drugs, motor vehicles, electrical appliances, and for specific places or activities, e.g., factories, mines, sports-grounds. The problem continually arose for the enforcement authorities that they could take no action in respect of a dangerous product for which there was no specific legislation. The move towards creating a generalised safety requirement began with the Consumer Protection Act 1961, replaced and extended by the Consumer Safety Act 1978 and again by the Consumer Protection Act 1987, Part II. This now provides that 'consumer goods' must comply with 'the general safety requirement' — a catch-all provision designed to close previous loopholes.

As we will see, there is a difference between the concept of 'defective' for the purposes of civil liability under Part I of CPA 1987, and failing to comply with 'the general safety requirement' under Part II. There are other differences regarding who is liable, product coverage, defences available. Why should this be? The Department of Trade and Industry's consultative[1] note explains:

> The main difference ... would be that the general safety requirement would be primarily enforced by criminal sanctions, whereas the Directive [i.e., CPA 1987, Part 1] imposes civil liability only. The government regard these two legislative measures on product safety as complementary. By making producers liable for putting unsafe products on the market, they both provide further incentives to the development, production and marketing of safer goods, thereby reducing the number and severity of accidents. The general safety requirement — backed by criminal sanctions — does this by requiring all suppliers, from manufacturers and importers to retailers, to exercise diligence in ensuring that the goods they supply meet sound modern standards of safety. The criminal sanctions are necessary to allow these standards to be enforced effectively, giving trading standards officers the powers to inspect goods for safety, to trace the source of unsafe goods and if necessary to remove them from the market. It is largely a preventive device, designed to secure the removal of unsafe products from the market at the earliest possible stage in the distribution process, before any accidents happen.
>
> Any criminal liability, particularly one based on the relative concept of safety and which can be imposed before a product causes any damage, must be based as far as possible on objective standards: the government have no wish to make criminals of suppliers who have taken all reasonable steps to ensure that their goods accord with sound modern standards. The requirement is therefore to be linked as far as possible with identifiable benchmarks, such as published British (or other) standards.
>
> Where such standards turn out to be defective or insufficient in any way, or where for any reason unsafe products do slip through the regulatory net, as is inevitable on occasions, it is reasonable for persons injured by such products to expect a facility for seeking compensation for their injuries. This is why a separate regime for *civil* liability is necessary. . . . Hence the two sets of liability, though having similar aims, approach the problems of safety from different angles. They are also very different in terms of product coverage ... and in the assessment of who is to be liable in different circumstances. Under the general safety requirement, for example, retailers are to be criminally liable if they knowingly expose an unsafe product for sale, whereas under the product liability regime retailers are liable (to third-party victims) in civil law if and only if they present themselves as the producer or cannot identify the person who supplied them with the product in question.

THE GENERAL SAFETY REQUIREMENT

By s. 10(1) in Part II of CPA 1987:

A person shall be guilty of an offence if he —

(a) supplies any consumer goods which fail to comply with the general safety requirement;

(b) offers or agrees to supply any such goods; or

(c) exposes or possesses any such goods for supply.

Contravention can result in a fine not exceeding £2,000, up to six months' imprisonment, or both.

Liability therefore rests on *any supplier*, not just on 'producers' (and those treated as if producers) who are civilly liable under Part I of the Act. 'Supply' is defined as including sale, hire, loan, hire-purchase, exchange, providing goods in connection with a statutory function (e.g., electricity), giving a prize or gift.[2] The 'person' need not be a trader, nor a trader supplying the type of goods he normally supplies. In theory, then, a private seller could be liable, but an exception is made for the sale of second-hand goods (see below), so this is unlikely in practice.

CPA 1987, s. 10(2), provides that:

For the purposes of this section consumer goods fail to comply with the general safety requirement if they are not reasonably safe having regard to all the circumstances, including —

(a) the manner in which, and purposes for which, the goods are being or would be marketed, the get-up of the goods, the use of any mark in relation to the goods and any instructions or warnings which are given or would be given with respect to the keeping, use or consumption of the goods;

(b) any standards of safety published by any person either for goods of a description which applies to the goods in question or for matters relating to goods of that description; and

(c) the existence of any means by which it would have been

reasonable (taking into account the cost, likelihood and extent of any improvement) for the goods to have been made safer.

This definition is very similar to that of 'defective' in Part I, and it might seem at this stage that no real difference exists between the two. However, the definitions of 'safe' and 'consumer goods' reveal that the criminal offence is more limited in scope than the civil requirement.

'Safe' is defined in terms of risk of causing death or personal injury only, whereas under Part I liability also arises for damage to personal property (exceeding £275). So, no criminal liability arises for goods which are only ever likely to cause property damage.

'Consumer goods' are defined by s. 10(7) as:

> . . . any goods which are ordinarily intended for *private* use or consumption, not being —

> (a)   growing crops or things comprised in land by virtue of being attached to it;

> (b)   water, food, feeding stuff or fertiliser;

> (c)   gas . . . supplied by a person authorised to supply it under . . . the Gas Act 1986;

> (d)   aircraft (other than hang-gliders) or motor vehicles;

> (e)   controlled drugs or licensed medicinal products;

> (f)   tobacco.

This is a much narrower definition than 'product' in Part I, excluding goods supplied for industrial or business purposes and a number of the potentially most dangerous goods for private use. However, when one takes account of other safety legislation the limitations are not significant:

● Exceptions (b) to (e) are already adequately covered by other statutes.

● Exception (f) recognises the difficulty of making the supply of tobacco a criminal offence.

● The limitation that 'consumer goods' must be for *private* use or consumption, whereas a 'product' can be supplied for any use, does not enable suppliers of industrial or business products to escape their responsibilities: the Health and Safety at Work etc. Act 1974 will apply (see pages 100–101).

However, exception (a) limits 'consumer goods' to things that are not attached to land, whereas 'product' under Part I does not (only primary agricultural produce and game, and land itself, is excluded).

Section 10(3) also lightens the general safety requirement by providing:

For the purposes of this section consumer goods shall not be regarded as failing to comply with the general safety requirement in respect of —

(a) anything which is shown to be attributable to compliance with any requirement imposed by or under any enactment or with any Community obligation.

This is identical to the defence provided in Part I. It will be recalled[3] that the risk must be directly attributable to compliance. However, s. 10(3) then goes further:

(b) any failure to do more in relation to any matter than is required by —

(i)   any safety regulations imposing requirements with respect to that matter;

(ii)   any standards of safety approved for the purposes of this subsection by or under any such regulations and imposing requirements with respect to that matter;

(iii) any provision of any enactment or subordinate legislation imposing such requirements with respect to that matter.

Meeting the *minimum* requirements of legislation or standards approved by regulations is therefore a complete defence in respect of criminal liability. It is not necessarily a defence to a civil claim, where the legislative standards are regarded as a minimum which ought, in certain circumstances, to be exceeded by the reasonably prudent producer (see pages 58–59).

Section 10(4) provides three further defences:

(a) that he reasonably believed that the goods would not be used or
     consumed in the United Kingdom.

This recognises that export goods may be made to different standards because
of the requirements of the importing country, which could render them unsafe
by UK standards, e.g., different electrical connectors and voltages.

(b) that the following conditions are satisfied, that is to say —

    (i)   that he supplied the goods, offered or agreed to supply them or
          . . . exposed or possessed them for supply in the course of
          carrying on a retail business; and

    (ii) that, at the time . . . he neither knew nor had reasonable grounds
          for believing that the goods failed to comply with the general
          safety requirement.

This is an important defence for the *retailer*, recognising that he may not have
the knowledge or resources to check whether the goods he sells meet the
general safety requirement. It should not be read as an excuse to carry out no
checks or ask no questions: the small corner shop selling a wide variety of
products would not be expected to carry out the sort of checks that a
supermarket chain or specialist dealer might be. A retailer should therefore take
note of the methods used by other similar retailers, and ensure that he keeps up
with them.

The defence applies only to retailers, not to others in the distribution chain such
as wholesalers and importers, or to manufacturers. However, there is another
defence of general application under s. 39, that of 'due diligence' (see pages
96–97).

(c) that the terms on which he supplied the goods or . . . intended to
     supply them —

    (i)   indicated that the goods were not supplied or to be supplied as
          new goods; and

    (ii) provided for, or contemplated, the acquisition of an interest in
          the goods by the persons supplied or to be supplied.

So, second-hand goods for *sale* are excluded, thereby effectively excluding most
private sales. These may be covered by specific safety regulations, but not by

the general safety requirement. The defence does not apply to goods which are *hired*, even if they are not brand new, because the person supplied does not acquire an interest in them. A tool hire business cannot therefore use this defence.

SAFETY REGULATIONS

By s. 11 the Secretary of State has power to issue safety regulations to ensure:

(a)   That goods are safe.

(b)   That goods which are unsafe, or would be unsafe in the hands of persons of a particular description, are not made available to persons generally or to persons of that description.

(c)   That appropriate information is, and inappropriate information is not, provided in relation to goods.

These regulations can cover such things as:

● Composition, design, construction, installation.

● Packaging.

● Testing, inspection to specified standards.

● Dealing with goods that do not satisfy the standard.

● Marks, warnings, instructions, other information to accompany goods.

● Prohibiting the supply of particular goods.

● Requiring information to be given to enforcement authorities.

Regulations already issued under the previous Consumer Protection Act 1961 and Consumer Safety Act 1978 are now subsumed by s. 11. The Secretary of State now has comprehensive powers to issue regulations covering all aspects of product safety. He does this by statutory instrument. This can take some time, because he must first consult organisations he considers are representative of interests which will be affected by a proposed regulation, and other appropriate persons.

A safety *regulation* is compulsory. Section 12 creates a number of criminal offences for breach, subject to the 'due diligence' defence, discussed below. An approved safety *standard* is not compulsory: failure to meet that standard is one of the circumstances to be considered in deciding whether a product meets the general safety requirement, but a supplier could argue that his product is safe enough even though it does not comply.

By s. 41 breach of a safety regulation (but not of the general safety requirement) is also grounds for a civil action by any person affected, i.e., for breach of statutory duty. This cannot be excluded or limited by any contract term or notice. A victim who suffers injury (but not property damage) from unsafe consumer goods which contravene a safety regulation can therefore sue under CPA 1987 both for the product being defective under Part I, and for breach of a regulation under Part II. In effect safety regulations become part of the definition of 'defective' in respect of personal injuries. A producer could face paying both damages to the victim and a fine to the State.

DUE DILIGENCE DEFENCE

An important general defence to breach of the general safety requirement and of safety regulations (and to certain other offences under the Act) is provided by s. 39:

> ... in proceedings against a person for an offence to which this section applies it shall be a defence for that person to show that he took all reasonable steps and exercised all due diligence to avoid committing the offence.

This could be by alleging that the offence was due —

> (a)   to the act or default of another; or

> (b)   to reliance on information given by another.

The defendant must identify or assist in the identification of that other person.

If the defence is based on reliance on information then he must show:

> ... that it was reasonable in all the circumstances for him to have relied on the information, having regard in particular —

> (a)   to the steps which he took, and those which might reasonably have been taken, for the purpose of verifying the information; and

(b)   to whether he had any reason to disbelieve the information.

This 'due diligence' defence represents the crucial difference between the concept of strict liability in contract and under Part I, and criminal liability under Part II: a producer may be liable to compensate a victim no matter how diligent he was or that someone else (e.g., a component supplier) was to blame.

This type of defence has been a common feature of consumer and employee protection legislation. The burden of proof is on the defendant, and is a heavy one. He must do more than show he acted naïvely or lacked experience. He will need to establish that he had some sort of system or procedure for checking safety, for training and supervising employees, for obtaining relevant information etc. For example, in a case[4] under the Trade Descriptions Act 1968, a dealer described a second-hand car as 'in good condition' without having checked it, simply relying on an MOT certificate. The car had corrosion, which had been partly hidden by undersealing. Donaldson LJ commented:

> ... the defendant had no system for ascertaining the condition of the vehicles being sold. He relied solely on MOT tests. . . . What he has to do is to show that it was a latent defect, that is to say, a defect which could not with reasonable diligence have been ascertained.

FURTHER POWERS AND ENFORCEMENT

Prohibition notice

In addition to the power under s. 11 to make regulations to prohibit the supply by *anyone* of a specified unsafe product, the Secretary of State has a further power under s. 13 to issue a 'prohibition notice' on a *named* person to prevent that person from supplying a product which the Secretary considers unsafe. This enables him to take prompt action against a particular trader to stop further supply of a particular product, without having to go through the lengthy procedure of consultation required before making a safety regulation. The trader has the right to make representations that the goods are safe and to have the notice revoked.

Notice to warn

The Secretary of State can serve on any person a 'notice to warn' requiring that person at his own expense to publish, in a form and manner and on occasions specified in the notice, a warning about any goods the Secretary considers are unsafe, which that person supplies or has supplied. The procedure requires a draft notice to be served, allowing the person 14 days to give notification of his intention to make representations to establish that the goods are safe and that the notice be withdrawn.

This power, first introduced by the Consumer Safety Act 1978, puts on a statutory basis a voluntary practice followed by certain reputable manufacturers and suppliers.[5] Apparently since 1978 it has never proved necessary to issue a notice to warn.

But there is no power to order a recall of unsafe goods.

While a person can be ordered to publish a notice to warn, with criminal prosecution for failure to comply, there is no power to order him to recall unsafe products. This may appear a shortcoming in the legislation, but it recognises three factors:

(a) Such a power is not necessary. As Lord Lucas, the government spokesman in the House of Lords during the passage of the 1987 legislation, observed:

It is significant that it has never proved necessary to serve a notice to warn as voluntary arrangements for removing unsafe goods from the market appear to work reasonably satisfactorily; and I believe that the power to prosecute suppliers for breach of the general safety requirement, coupled with the enhanced enforcement powers, renders even more remote the prospect of having to serve such a notice, let alone needing recourse to a mandatory recall power. The threat of being told to publish a public notice stating that the goods are unsafe and that the Secretary of State is making you tell people is extremely persuasive.

(b) The difficulty of prescribing how a recall should be conducted, given the problems of who to contact, the method of communication, what to do if there is no response etc. With the vast majority of consumer sales there is no record of the name and address of the first purchaser, let alone subsequent users. Even when guarantee or registration cards are provided, people fail to return them. Motor vehicles are the only consumer product with a compulsory registration system to enable current owners to be traced, and that is never 100% accurate.

(c) If a producer does not make every effort to recall, then defective goods will continue in circulation which, if they result in injury or damage, will render him liable to civil action by victims. This could prove far more expensive than any fine. His reputation and sales will no doubt also suffer, and his insurance premium rise.

Suspension notice

Section 14 enables an enforcement authority (e.g., trading standards officer), which has reasonable grounds for suspecting that any safety provision relating to any goods has been contravened, to serve a notice prohibiting the person for up to six months from supplying, offering or exposing for supply those goods.

This is another means of taking prompt action to prevent unsafe goods getting into circulation. It may be followed by a prosecution. There are provisions for the trader to appeal to a magistrates' court against the notice and to obtain compensation if there has in fact been no contravention.

Forfeiture

Section 16 provides a more drastic power for an enforcement authority to obtain possession of unsafe goods and, if necessary, destroy them. The procedure requires the authority to apply first to a magistrates' court on grounds that there has been a contravention of a safety provision. This may be inferred from the fact that other goods of the same design or batch have been found to contravene a provision. If the court is satisfied, it issues a forfeiture order. This may specify that the goods be destroyed, or released only to someone in the business of repairing or scrapping such goods.

A person affected by a forfeiture order may appeal to a Crown Court to have it withdrawn or delayed.

Power to obtain information

The Secretary of State can require any person to supply him with information, including records, to help him make decisions regarding safety regulations, prohibition notices and notices to warn. Failure to comply, or supplying false information is an offence.

Other enforcement powers

Part IV contains provisions giving various powers to an enforcement authority;

(a)   To make test purchases.

(b)   To enter and search premises.

(c)   To examine procedures for producing and testing goods.

(d)   To examine, copy or detain records.

(e)   To seize and detain goods.

(f)   To require containers or vending machines to be opened.

Customs officers can seize any imported goods and detain them for up to two days for checks by an enforcement authority.

Obstructing an enforcement officer is an offence. A trader visited by an officer should therefore be cooperative, but first seek explanation why the visit is being made and then try to delay the examination until legal representation has been sought.   .

CRIMINAL LIABILITY FOR NON-CONSUMER GOODS

Goods which are supplied for non-consumer use are outside the criminal provisions of CPA 1987. The majority of such goods will be covered by the Health and Safety at Work etc. Act (HASAWA) 1974.

This Act imposes a wide range of duties to ensure the health, safety and welfare of persons at work; to protect persons other than those at work against risks to health and safety arising from the activities of persons at work and from the use of non-domestic premises; to control explosives and other dangerous substances, and emissions of offensive substances into the atmosphere. It extends to fairground equipment.

So far as liability for products supplied for use at work or in non-domestic premises is concerned, the general duty is laid down by s. 6 as amended.[6]

This obliges any person who designs, manufactures, imports or supplies any *article* for use at work or any article of fairground equipment to ensure, *so far as is reasonably practicable,* that the article is safe and without risk to health. This applies to machinery, equipment, tools and such items, both new and second-hand. A similar duty applies to manufacturers, importers and suppliers of *substances* for use at work or in non-domestic premises (e.g., launderettes).

'Safe' refers to risk of personal injury, not damage to property.

The duty includes:

● Ensuring that the article is designed and constructed to be safe and without risk to health when being set, used, cleaned or maintained by a person at work; similarly that fairground equipment is safe for entertainment of the public.

● Ensuring that substances will be safe and without risk to health when being handled, processed, stored or transported by persons at work.

● Carrying out necessary testing and examination for the above purposes.

● Providing adequate information about the safe use of the article or substance, which may include the results of tests.

● Providing revisions of such information when a risk becomes known.

● When designing or manufacturing a relevant article, to carry out necessary research to discover and, so far as is reasonably practicable, eliminate or minimise risks to health or safety.

● When installing or erecting a relevant article, to ensure that nothing about the way it is installed or erected makes it unsafe or a risk to health.

Failure to fulfil these duties is a criminal offence, punishable by unlimited fines and up to two years' imprisonment. Health and safety inspectors have powers to enter premises, make tests etc. similar to those given to enforcement authorities by CPA 1987. They can issue prohibition notices to stop unsafe items being supplied and used, and improvement notices to require changes to be made.

In s. 6 (and throughout the HASAWA 1974) terms such as 'so far as is reasonably practicable' and 'reasonable care' appear. This is the same test as for establishing negligence for civil liability, so effectively the Act makes failure to take reasonable care into a criminal offence in respect of the goods, persons and places covered.

OTHER PRODUCTS NOT COVERED BY THE GENERAL SAFETY REQUIREMENT OR BY SAFETY REGULATIONS ISSUED UNDER THE CONSUMER PROTECTION ACT 1987.

There remain several categories of product for which separate provision is made.

Food is governed primarily by the Food Act 1984. All the detailed control of the composition, preparation and sale of food is to be found in numerous subordinate regulations, much of it deriving from EC requirements.

The Act broadly seeks to ensure that food and milk are safe for human consumption. Regulations require the addition or prohibit the use of certain ingredients and substances; require the use of certain methods of treatment or processing; and specify the composition generally of particular types of food. The latter is usually done by prescribing minimum or maximum percentages of particular ingredients and additives. Various offences arise through failure to meet these standards.

Further offences arise where a person supplies food unfit for human consumption, through being adulterated, putrid, dirty etc. It is a defence to show that adequate notice was given that the food was not intended for human consumption.

It can also be an offence to sell food which is fit for consumption, but not of the nature, substance or quality demanded by the purchaser, e.g., he asked for concentrated orange juice but was sold a diluted form. The obvious defence is that of informing the purchaser that the item falls below the standard he might reasonably expect. Where a substance has been added or abstracted, or the food processed or treated in some way, but it has not thereby become injurious to health, then it is a defence to show that the operation was not carried out fraudulently and that a conspicuous notice was attached stating the nature of the operation, e.g., 'Contains 10% . . .'.

Where extraneous matter is present in food, it is a defence to show that this was an 'unavoidable consequence of the process of collection or preparation'. This is very hard to prove. In *Smedleys Ltd* v *Breed*,[7] a caterpillar was found in a can of peas. It might well have been harmless if eaten, but clearly rendered the peas not of the substance demanded. The defendant canning company showed it had produced over 3.5 million cans during the year and, thanks to its excellent quality systems, there had only been four complaints of the presence of extraneous matter. It argued that it would have been impractical to have done any more to seek to eliminate such extraneous matter; that in any process there will be occasional failures. The company was not negligent, but nevertheless it was found guilty of an offence because the presence of the caterpillar was not an *unavoidable* consequence of the canning process.

The case also illustrates the defence of 'act or default of another': the store which sold the offending can was able to escape criminal liability by blaming the canners. The store might, of course, face civil liability under the Sale of Goods Act 1979 for selling goods not of merchantable quality, or unfit for the particular purpose, or even misdescribing them!

Fertilisers, pesticides, seeds, animal feed etc. which can affect the safety of food for human consumption, or of the environment, are similarly tightly regulated.[8]

Drugs and medicines need special regulation because a 'general safety requirement' would be impossible to determine. Drugs have side effects, sometimes very dangerous ones, but the risk is normally worthwhile because of the possible benefits. The misuse of drugs obviously presents another problem in determining the nature of any liability of the producer or supplier.

The Medicines Act 1968 and subordinate regulations control 'medicinal products', defined broadly as any substance or article other than an instrument, apparatus or appliance to be administered to human beings or animals for a medicinal purpose. These cover promoting, labelling and packaging; leaflets and advertising; standards and permitted ingredients (as laid down in the British Pharmacopoeia or other approved compendia). Different labelling requirements apply to drugs available without prescription, with more details on ingredients, dosages, warnings about side effects etc. than for prescribed drugs.

Offences are broadly similar to those under food regulations.

The appropriate minister has power to prohibit the sale, supply or importation of medicinal products of any kind if it appears necessary in the interests of safety.

Tight control over drugs is exercised by requiring producers and suppliers to hold a relevant licence. The licensing authority (a body of health ministers and agriculture ministers) oversees the granting, renewal, variation etc. of licences. It must be satisfied that there has been adequate research and testing, that the manufacturer has adequate resources and quality control systems to ensure safety and quality, and that the drug has a positive value, before issuing a product licence. Wholesaler's and manufacturer's licences must also be obtained, ensuring that others in the chain of supply are vetted. Appropriate exemptions are made for qualified doctors, dentists, pharmacists etc. who make up a particular preparation for a patient.

The Misuse of Drugs Act 1971 lists those drugs considered particularly dangerous in three controlled categories, A, B and C. It restricts the production, supply, import and export of these to authorised persons, with strict controls on custody, markings and other measures to prevent misuse.

Other statutes

Largely for historical reasons a number of potentially dangerous products are regulated by their own statutes rather than safety regulations under CPA 1987. These include explosives, poisons, petroleum and furniture fillings.[9]

Motor vehicles and their accessories (including motor cycle protective helmets) are subject to highly specialised legislation.[10]

Aircraft are subject to both international conventions and national legislation.[11] The main safeguard is that civil aircraft require a 'certificate of airworthiness' issued by the Civil Aviation Authority before being allowed to fly.

Gas, electricity and water by their nature require separate legislation from normal consumer goods. The authorities responsible for these utilities have been created by statute. Quality standards are controlled first by restricting who can make supplies to the authorities themselves or those approved and monitored by them. Secondly by provisions requiring them to provide and maintain supplies to specified standards. The Authorities are largely self-regulatory. While they can incur criminal liabilities, it is unusual for prosecutions to be brought,[12] except privately by conservation groups and campaigners. It is more appropriate for the relevant minister to take action to remedy the problem. This policy may change with privatisation.

The pipes, wires, fittings, appliances etc. used to connect the supply are subject to numerous regulations in the same way as other potentially dangerous products.

WHO IS LIABLE FOR AN OFFENCE — THE INDIVIDUAL OR THE ORGANISATION HE WORKS FOR?

It was noted in chapter 4 that an employer will be vicariously liable for the civil wrongs committed by employees. The issue is not so simple for criminal liability. The general rule is that an employer will *not* be vicariously liable for his employee's crimes. Thus if an employee driving a company car on company business is convicted of speeding, he will incur the penalties, not his employer.

Under the HASAWA 1974 prosecutions can be (and are) taken against individual employees responsible for the offence. If, for example, a sales representative fails to pass on safety information then he can be prosecuted. So too can his company, irrespective of whether the individual is prosecuted (s. 36(1)).

However, under various other Acts where the offence consists of 'selling' or 'being in possession of' some product, the employer commits the crime, not the employee actually arranging the sale or physically holding the product. The essence of a 'sale' is a transfer of property from A to B, and it is A's property rather than his employee's that is being sold. The employer therefore can have committed an offence of 'selling', even though he was nowhere near the place at the time of sale.[13]

Offences under CPA 1987 generally consist of 'supplying', so the principle cannot quite so readily be applied. It may, therefore, be possible for the employee to be prosecuted. In practice the enforcement authorities will invariably proceed against the employer, not the individual employee causing the offence.

The 'person' accused (a company is legally a 'person') can try to escape liability by pointing to the act or default of another, e.g., an outsider *or* an employee. The employer would have to show that 'he took all reasonable steps and exercised all due diligence' in the circumstances by proper training and instructions to staff, supervision, management structures, systems of work etc. This will be difficult to prove, but by no means impossible.[14] Whether it is justified to allow the employer to escape liability in this way has been the subject of much debate and of a Law Commission investigation.[15]

In the case of a company, conceptual difficulties arise in attributing to it motives, intentions or any other physical and mental activity. It can only act through living persons, and the question arises as to which of those persons are to be treated as acting *as* the company, and which as separate individuals on whom the default can be blamed:

> Normally the board of directors, the managing director and perhaps other superior officers of a company carry out the functions of management and speak and act as the company. Their subordinates do not. They carry out orders from above and it can make no difference that they are given some measure of discretion. But the board of directors may delegate some part of their functions of management giving to their delegate full discretion to act independently of instructions from them. I see no difficulty in holding that they have thereby put such a delegate in their place so that within the scope of the delegation he can act as the company. It may not always be easy to draw the line but there are cases in which the line must be drawn.[16]

In the case in question a shop manager of a large supermarket chain with considerable managerial powers was nevertheless held to be 'another person', allowing the company to escape liability for a breach of the Trade Descriptions Act 1968 when a misleading price offer was displayed due to his failure to check it.

> . . . here the board never delegated any part of their functions. They set up a chain of command through regional and district supervisors, but they remained in control. The shop managers had to obey their general directions and also take orders from their superiors. The acts or omissions of shop managers were not acts of the company itself.

> . . . the appellants established the statutory defence.

So, if the employer can escape liability, does this make the employee liable to prosecution?

Section 40(1) of CPA 1987 provides:

> Where the commission by any person of an offence . . . is due to an act or default committed by some other person in the course of any business of his, the other person shall be guilty of the offence and may be proceeded against and punished . . . whether or not proceedings are taken against the first-mentioned person.

The key to interpretation is whether 'business of *his*' refers to the first person (i.e., employer) or the other person (employee). There seems little doubt that it means the other person, so an employee will not be proceeded against because he is not a business. It would only apply where that 'other person' is carrying on his own business, e.g., an independent supplier or sub-contractor.

Whatever the interpretation of this badly drafted section, the decision to prosecute is with the enforcement authorities, and their policy is generally not to seek to punish employees.

Directors and officers of a company do not enjoy such protection. By s. 40(2):

> Where a body corporate is guilty of an offence . . . in respect of any act or default which is shown to have been committed with the consent or connivance of, or to be attributable to any neglect on the part of, any director, manager, secretary or other similar officer of the body corporate or any person who was purporting to act in any such capacity he, as well as the body corporate, shall be guilty of that offence and shall be liable to be proceeded against and punished accordingly.

Punishment is by fine and/or imprisonment. Two separate offences have been committed, so two fines can be imposed. A company cannot go to gaol, but a director can!

AVOIDING CRIMINAL LIABILITY

The duties imposed by safety legislation are by their nature rigorous. Few defences are available if a breach occurs. Where a defence is based on 'due diligence', 'all practicable steps,' reasonable care' and similar notions, the burden of proof is on the accused. Most of the offences do not require *mens rea*, i.e., a guilty mind, so can be committed without any intention, recklessness or even knowledge that a regulation has been broken.

The first step in avoidance is to find out precisely what regulations and standards exist. This does not necessarily mean access to a law library or keeping an up-to-date copy of *Halsbury's Laws of England*. Copies of individual statutes and statutory instruments are available through government bookshops. British Standards can be obtained from BSI Sales Department.[17]

Information and copies of explanatory leaflets can be sought from the Department of Trade and Industry.[18]

Locally advice can be sought from the relevant enforcement authority, i.e., the Trading Standards Department or Health and Safety Executive. By seeking such advice and following recommendations, it is unlikely they will be minded to prosecute if a breach inadvertently occurs. In the writer's experience officers from these authorities are loath to bring a prosecution if it can be avoided, if only because of the time and paperwork involved. They prefer to educate, advise and warn.

If a prosecution is brought for an offence then, in the absence of any defence, a plea in mitigation can be made. This will benefit from the existence of a previous good safety record, high standards, rigorous quality control systems, and other evidence that efforts have been made to minimise risks. The penalty may then be no more than a small fine.

Criticism is sometimes made at the derisory fines imposed, even for a flagrant breach of the regulations. Most of the offences carry a maximum fine of £2,000, which is hardly going to hurt a large company. What hurts more is the publicity and its effect on reputation and sales.

SUMMARY

Criminal liability in respect of defective products arises through breach of duties imposed by safety legislation. The most important source is now the Consumer Protection Act 1987, Part II. This creates two broad categories of liability:

(a)   Failure to comply with the general safety requirement with respect to consumer goods.

(b)   Breach of safety regulations.

The Health and Safety at Work etc. Act 1974 creates liabilities for those supplying products for industrial or business use. Other legislation covers categories of product not within the ambit of these two acts, e.g., food, drugs, motor vehicles.

The aim of the legislation is primarily to prevent accidents. Penalties can be imposed without anyone having suffered injury. Where injury has resulted, the producer may face both criminal and civil liability.

NOTES

1   Department of Trade and Industry, *Implementation of EC Directive on Product
Liability: An Explanatory and Consultative Note* (London: Department of Trade
and Industry, 1985).

2   CPA 1987, s.46.

3   CPA 1987, s. 4(1)(a). See chapter 3.

4   *Barker* v *Hargreaves* [1981] RTR 197.

5   For example, the Code of Practice of Action Concerning Vehicle Safety
Defects, agreed between members of the Society of Motor Manufacturers and
Traders.

6   The amendments to s. 6 are in CPA 1987, sch. 3.

7   [1974] AC 839.

8   For example, by the Plant Varieties and Seeds Act 1964, Plant Health Act
1967, Agriculture (Miscellaneous Provisions) Act 1972, Farm and Garden
Chemicals Act 1967.

9   Explosives Acts 1875 and 1923 and the Explosives (Age of Purchase etc.)
Act 1976; Poisons Act 1972; Petroleum (Consolidation) Act 1928; Rag, Flock
and Other Filling Materials Act 1951.

10   The principal Act is the Road Traffic Act 1972, under which most
regulations are made. Most safety aspects are contained in the Road Vehicles
(Construction and Use) Regulations 1986 (SI 1986/1078), which are continually
being amended.

11   Air Navigation Order 1985 (SI 1985/1643).

12   At the time of writing a prosecution is being considered against the South
West Water Authority in respect of contamination of supplies in the Camelford
area.

13   *Coppen* v *Moore (No. 2)* [1898] 2 QB 306. For a full discussion of the
principle see J.C. Smith and B. Hogan, *Criminal Law*, 6th ed. (London:
Butterworths, 1988), ch. 8.

14   *Tesco Supermarkets Ltd* v *Nattrass* [1971] AC 153.

15   Law Commission, *Codification of the Criminal Law: General Principles: Criminal Liability of Corporations* (Working Paper No. 44) (London: HMSO, 1972).

16   Per Lord Reid in *Tesco Supermarkets Ltd* v *Nattrass* [1972] AC 153 at p. 171.

17   BSI Sales Department, Linford Wood, Milton Keynes MK14 6LE, telephone Milton Keynes (0908) 221166, who will also advise on other sales outlets.

18   Department of Trade and Industry, Consumer Safety Unit, 10–18 Victoria Street, London SW1H 0NN, telephone 01-215 7877.

PART II
MANAGING THE PRODUCT LIABILITY RISK

6

Defects

The basis of product liability is proof that the product was in some way defective and that this led to the loss or injury complained of.

Loss or injury sustained through using a product which is not 'defective' in any of these ways cannot give rise to a civil claim, except in very few parts of the world where an 'absolute liability' system operates. New Zealand has such a system, victims being paid from a State insurance fund.

The 'defect' must have existed at the time of supply and be the proximate cause of the accident, in whole or part. The producer or supplier can therefore be relieved of some or all liability (under most jurisdictions) through the contributory fault of the user (e.g., misuse) or someone else who has intervened (e.g., the dealer failing to carry out proper servicing).

Three types of defect

For practical purposes a product may be considered 'defective' under any one of three headings:

(a) A manufacturing defect — where it was not produced or constructed as intended.

(b) A design defect — where it was produced entirely in accordance with the specification, but is nevertheless unreasonably dangerous.

(c) A warning or instruction defect — where it is unreasonably dangerous due to the inadequacy of warnings and/or instructions for use.

MANUFACTURING DEFECT

Typical examples of manufacturing defects are where the manufacturer uses faulty materials, deviates from the proper specification or production process, or fails to test adequately during production.

A manufacturer can be liable not only for the parts he makes, but also any bought-in materials incorporated into the product. The responsibility for ensuring that defects do not occur therefore extends beyond his own manufacturing system to his supplier quality assurance system.

Consequences of a manufacturing defect

Usually only an isolated product or batch is affected by a manufacturing defect, so any liability will be limited to damage caused by these. Remedial action is by way of a recall, rectification or warning for the batch affected, and a review of production processes to prevent recurrence.

If the defect is in a bought-in component, then contractual recourse can be sought against the component supplier, or he can be joined as co-defendant. It is important to ensure that the terms of purchase allow for recourse, i.e., that the supplier has not excluded or limited his liability (see chapter 2).

To minimise the impact, careful records should be kept. Can those finished products fitted with the faulty batch of components or made from the defective ingredients be traced? How many went through the faulty process? Which machine or operator was responsible? Are components or finished products numbered or dated for easier identification? These matters are discussed in chapters 8 and 9.

What must the manufacturer do to ensure he is not liable for manufacturing defects?

Simple: prevent them occurring!

Under strict liability principles it is not a question of taking reasonable care to minimise the chances of a defect slipping through. *To avoid legal liability there must be no defects.* So, having excellent systems, standards and an untarnished reputation for producing defect-free products will not in themselves protect the manufacturer, nor will the argument that it was a one-in-million freak occurrence.

The defence offered by CPA 1987 is the problematic s. 4(1)(e):

> that the state of scientific and technical knowledge at the relevant time was
> not such that a producer of products of the same description as the product in
> question might be expected to have discovered the defect if it had existed in
> his products while they were under his control.

The limits of this defence have already been discussed in chapter 3. In summary, it is designed to protect producers at the forefront of technology, such as drug and aircraft manufacturers. We await the first test cases to see how the courts interpret the defence, but it would seem that for the vast majority of manufacturers it is unlikely to apply: it can virtually always be argued that a producer of similar products 'might' be expected to have discovered the defect by applying better technology. Normally if a producer spent enough time, effort and money he might have discovered the defect: the defect slips through because he is not prepared to go to such lengths. It may be technologically feasible to test every component and process on every item produced, but not commercially realistic. Instead there will be 100% testing of certain components and processes, or of complete assemblies rather than each component part, and sample testing of others.

In the real world it is therefore a matter of *minimising* the chances of defects. A commercial decision has to be taken by balancing the degree of risk, likelihood of occurrence and cost of prevention against the possible direct and indirect costs of product liability actions.

Deviating from the design specification

It is not always possible for the manufacturing arm to follow the designer's specification. This can occur because the specification is impractical: the designer's ideas cannot be put into practice because they simply don't work (e.g., the 2-D drawing cannot be translated into 3-D reality); or they are unnecessarily difficult; or the available machinery, materials or operators are unsuitable to meet the specification.

This should be sorted out during pre-production feasibility studies.

Once production starts, there may be:

(a)   shortages of the correct materials, breakdowns of machinery or non-availability of trained operators;

(b)   corner cutting due to poor supervision, apathy, time or cost-saving, the pressure to meet production targets, or the operator thinking he knows a better way.

In all such cases the danger is that the alternative method has not been properly tested or approved. Even where a procedure exists for seeking approval of the deviation (by raising a 'concession'), the pressures of meeting production targets, time and cost may tempt employees to ignore it.

If this leads to a defect, then not only would the producer be strictly liable: he has set a standard and by his own admission failed to achieve it, so additionally could be:

(a)   negligent;

(b)   reckless, which in the USA could mean punitive damages;

(c)   committing a criminal offence, with no hope of using the defence that he 'exercised all due diligence'.

The pressures and temptations to take such chances can be great; the consequences could be catastrophic!

The solution therefore is to have strictly enforced procedures that require all changes to be approved. Careful records should be maintained of which products were manufactured with the deviation in case they need to be traced for remedial action.

Quality control

Consistent quality can only be achieved by adhering to strict quality control systems. It is beyond the scope of this book to detail these. Guidance can be found from British Standards, e.g.,

Quality Assurance   BS 4891 : 1972
Quality Control Systems   BS 5179 : 1974
Quality Systems   BS 5750 : 1981

and from other standards such as Defence Standard 05-21, 05-26.

BS 5750 is a national standard for managing the quality of manufacturing procedures. It sets out how companies can establish, document and maintain an effective and economic system for developing and maintaining the quality of their products. It is subject to independent audit and certification.

Appendix 1 shows a list of questions which indicate its scope.

Increasingly commercial purchasers are insisting as a condition of purchase that their suppliers meet these standards.

DESIGN DEFECT

Typical examples of design defects are found in products constructed with materials of insufficient strength or durability, products where general design specification exposes consumers to unreasonable dangers, or products which lack appropriate safety features.

The consequences of a design defect can be crippling: massive recalls, costly modifications, loss of reputation and sales, even going out of business. Once one victim has successfully sued, there could be a bandwagon effect, as happened with the 'unintended acceleration' claims in America against certain vehicle manufacturers: a design defect was genuinely to blame for some accidents when cars suddenly accelerated out of the driver's control, but thereafter other drivers crashing for whatever reason made the same allegation.

Even under a strict liability regime it is necessary to show that a reasonably prudent manufacturer would not have designed and put the product into circulation in that form had he known of the risk. CPA 1987 puts this in terms of what 'persons generally are entitled to expect'. The Sale of Goods Act 1979 defines 'merchantable quality' in terms of what it is 'reasonable to expect in the circumstances'.

The American experience of strict liability is a useful guide to the likely interpretation that English courts will give to CPA 1987 and a number of American cases will be used as illustrations.

The court has to weigh up the utility of the product as designed against its impaired utility from a redesign to alleviate the danger. The plaintiff has to show that there was a suitable alternative design in terms of technological feasibility, cost and practicality, and that had it been used the loss or injury would not have occurred. Was the product *unreasonably dangerous* for its intended purpose?

This balancing act is illustrated in the following vehicle cases. In the first[1] a 1968

Volkswagen Microbus hit a telephone pole at 40 m.p.h. The American court observed:

> It may be that in every case the injuries may be somewhat different, but any 'head-on' collision at a speed of 40 miles an hour or more will result in severe injuries to the occupants of a vehicle and, certainly in 1968, no design short of an impractical and exorbitantly expensive tank-like vehicle . . . could have protected against such injuries; in fact, it is doubtful that even such a vehicle could have.

The court noted several factors to be considered:

(a)   the defect's obviousness;

(b)   the vehicle's purposes, including design, utility, style, attractiveness and marketability;

(c)   the vehicle's price and, in particular, the effect which added safety features would have upon the price relative to marketability; and

(d)   the circumstances of the particular collision.

In another car crash case[2] it was noted:

> . . . if a change in design would add little to safety, render the vehicle ugly or inappropriate for its particular purpose, and add a small fortune to the purchase price, then a court should rule as a matter of law that the manufacturer had not created an unreasonable risk of harm.

Compare this with a case where a vehicle was involved in a head-on collision and the occupants were badly burned. The fuel pipe was ruptured in the crash but the fuel pump continued to feed fuel to the fire. This could have been prevented by fitting an inertia cut-off switch into the fuel system. There was no legal requirement for such a switch, but it was fitted by other manufacturers of similar vehicles, and indeed by this manufacturer on other models, i.e., the technology existed and was feasible, but the manufacturer chose not to use it. The American court awarded punitive damages against the manufacturer.

As explained in chapter 3, the fact that a product is not in breach of a regulation does not necessarily mean that there can be no legal liability. Too often designers make the mistake that compliance with regulations is automatically good enough — it may not be.

Of particular interest to vehicle manufacturers are those actions where courts have had to consider whether there is a duty to design a vehicle not simply to avoid causing an accident but also to protect occupants when involved in one. This is known as the 'second collision theory' or 'crashworthiness doctrine'.

Most US States now follow the 1968 decision in *Larsen* v *G.M.*[3] in which it was held that:

> Where the manufacturer's negligence in design causes an unreasonable risk to be imposed upon the user of its products, the manufacturer should be liable for the injury caused by its failure to exercise reasonable care in the design. These injuries are readily foreseeable as an incident to the normal and expected use of an automobile. While automobiles are not made for the purpose of colliding with each other, a frequent and inevitable contingency of normal automobile use will result in collisions and injury-producing impacts. No rational basis exists for limiting recovery to situations where the defect in design or manufacture was the causative factor of the accident, as the accident and the resulting injury, usually caused by the so-called 'second collision' of the passenger with the interior part of the automobile, all are foreseeable. . . . The sole function of an automobile is not just to provide a means of transportation, it is to provide a means of safe transportation or as safe as is reasonably possible under the present state of the art.

The crashworthiness doctrine has been applied not just to occupants of various forms of vehicle, but also to pedestrians, cyclists etc., colliding with vehicles (e.g., being injured by dangerous protruding hub-caps), and to other products, e.g., in one case[4] to a lamp-post which fell on to pedestrians after being hit by a car. It is basically an extension of the foreseeability principle, and while some of the court decisions may appear harsh for the manufacturer, there is no logical reason why he should not design the product to perform safely in foreseeable accidents as well as to avoid causing them.

Design philosophy and practice

Designers must be constantly aware of developments in technology and in the standards required by law arising out of legislation and court decisions. Over the next few years the latter will be vital, with British and European courts giving their interpretation of the new legislation.

Remember that most legislative standards are minima: while compliance may avoid committing a criminal offence, the test for civil liability is not that the product scrapes through the standard, but how much it exceeds it, given the state of the art at the time.

Suppose a minimum strength or thickness of some material is laid down by a regulation: should the producer double the strength or thickness, which is technologically feasible but would double the price? The answer can only be found by referring to the definition of 'defect', i.e., the level of safety which 'persons generally are entitled to expect'. All the circumstances have to be taken into account, of which cost is just one. The industry standard is a powerful indicator, but not an absolute test: the court might find that all manufacturers of similar products are failing to meet current expectations.

Good design practice does not simply mean trying to design the product so that it will not fail, but identifying how it *might* fail and with what consequences. Allowance has to be made for the foreseeable events during the life of the product such as wear and tear, lack of maintenance or service, misuse and even what happens when it is thrown away (e.g., pressurised cans).

The 'product' means what is supplied to the user, so includes packaging.

There are various techniques to achieve this, of which only a few can be briefly mentioned in a book of this scope.[5]

The simplest involves sitting people, preferably including some from outside the company or design team, round a table asking awkward and even silly questions: 'What if . . .?', 'Could this ever . . .?', 'Why . . .?' The team needs at least one person prepared to make an idiot of himself by raising these matters: too often the people closely involved fail to spot the obvious.

A more sophisticated version of this is called the Delphi method. This can take various forms, but in essence is a method of taking the opinions of a group of experts to reach a conclusion where hard facts are unobtainable. Each expert is asked to predict (usually on a questionnaire) the probability and severity of a particular hazard. By refining the results a consensus can sometimes be reached and decisions made. A scoring system can be used (very low probability/ severity = 1, very high = 5). Multiplying the scores gives a risk index which can enable the manufacturer to identify and tackle the most serious problems first.

Other techniques include fault tree analysis (FTA) and failure modes and effects analysis (FMEA). FTA involves selecting a possible undesirable event, such as a fire in an engine, and then identifying a logical combination of the circumstances that could produce that event. A diagram in the form of a family tree can be drawn, showing different routes by which the event could arise. The critical combinations can then be identified and action taken to prevent them so combining.

FMEA involves identifying all known and potential failure modes, their causes and effects. It uses a ranking system (usually scoring 1–10) to rate factors such as probability of occurrence, severity of failure, likelihood of detection before damage is caused. Multiplying the scores gives a risk priority number. If this is below a predetermined level then no action may be considered necessary; the higher the number the more urgent the corrective action.

New technology and safety features

The term 'defective' takes into account the time when the product was supplied. Technology advances, new safety features and manufacturing processes become available, and with them the 'consumer expectation' rises.

This does not mean that as soon as one producer comes up with a safer feature all others must immediately follow suit. If that were the case then every product would have to be made to the highest possible safety specification and cost an exorbitant amount, which would not be acceptable to consumers. The consumer also expects a choice, both of price and design. One lawn-mower manufacturer might produce a model with plastic safety blades, so the user can happily run over his feet without injury. Does this make a mower with metal blades defective? Probably not, since the metal has advantages such as longer life, more rugged application etc., and is not dangerous if operated correctly. The instructions and warnings may need to be reviewed: previously no one expected to be able to run over their feet without injury; now perhaps if most mowers have safety blades the expectation changes, and a warning becomes necessary because the danger is no longer so obvious. (See 'Warnings' below.)

Faced with changing technology what should the producer do?

● Check what the other producers are doing.

● Continually review the safety of the product, avoiding the blinkered approach of 'We've been making it like that for years'.

● Carry out proper assessments of the latest features.

● Document the results, particularly the reasons for not adopting a new feature, ensuring that cost does not dominate.

The lawyers will ask the question: 'Did you consider this alternative?'

The producer needs to be able to respond: 'Yes, and these are the reasons why we thought it was not appropriate'.

WARNING OR INSTRUCTION DEFECT

A product may be 'defective' if there is no warning, or an inadequate warning, of the dangers associated with it, or no or inadequate instructions about its safe use.[6]

Warnings are needed where the danger exceeds what the user might reasonably expect. The two questions to be asked are:

(a)   Is the product unreasonably dangerous?

(b)   Would the warning have prevented the loss or injury?

It may sometimes be the case that no warning can prevent the product being dangerous other than 'Don't use it'. But the utility factor may outweigh the danger, so the producer's duty is to ensure the user is fully aware of the dangers and can take steps to minimise the risk. Sometimes the danger is so obvious that no warning is necessary — the user simply assumes the risks when he chooses the product, e.g., a knife, chainsaw etc.

Instructions seek to ensure safe and appropriate use. While this can be viewed as a separate function from warnings, the law makes no distinction, applying the same rules to both. ('Warning' will henceforth be taken as including 'instruction'.)

What must the producer do to ensure he adequately warns or instructs?

For many categories of goods there are specific regulations regarding warnings. The Classification, Packaging and Labelling of Dangerous Substances Regulations 1984 (SI 1984/1244) and accompanying codes of practice cover numerous substances classified by the Health and Safety Executive as dangerous, both for supply and transportation by road. The labelling must include specified words and symbols to indicate hazards and precautions. The packaging must be designed to prevent leakage during normal handling.

Further regulations, mainly resulting from EEC legislation, apply to specific products, e.g., the Asbestos Products (Safety) Regulations 1985 (SI 1985/2042 amended by 1987/1979) require any product containing asbestos to carry the specified warning label. Drugs available without prescription require information on ingredients, quantity, use, side effects and various other matters.[7] Certain categories of food have to be supplied with details of composition, additives, methods of process and treatment etc.[8] Breach of these requirements is a criminal offence, and may also be grounds for a civil action.

More generally the Health and Safety at Work etc. Act 1974, s. 6, requires designers, manufacturers, importers or suppliers of any article for use at work or any article of fairground equipment to take such steps as are necessary to secure that persons supplied with the article are provided with adequate safety information.

With regard to consumer goods, CPA 1987 extends the powers of the Secretary of State to issue regulations, including prohibitions on the supply of goods without proper warnings, requiring traders to publish warnings about unsafe goods already on the market, and enabling enforcement authorities to issue suspension notices to prevent continued supply (see chapter 5).

In addition there are industry standards, codes and guidelines. While not mandatory, non-observance would invariably be sufficient grounds for a civil claim.

Clearly a producer or supplier should obtain copies of the regulations, codes of practice and any explanatory information. The burden is on him to find out and apply the current requirements. Pleading ignorance or misunderstanding of regulations would not suffice unless 'he took all reasonable steps and exercised all due diligence to avoid committing the offence'.

Beyond the specific rules the adequacy of a warning is a matter of applying the general principles of foreseeability, practicality and balancing of risks, i.e., the 'consumer expectation test'.

The duty covers three related aspects:

(a)   to warn users of the hazards associated with the product;

(b)   to instruct users on the safe uses, operation and maintenance of the product;

(c)   to inform of the consequences of failure to heed those warnings and instructions.

An example is the case of *Devilez* v *Boots Pure Drug Co. Ltd*,[9]. in which the plaintiff suffered injury from corn solvent. Having taken a bath and applied some of this to his feet, he was putting the bottle away when it tipped over, the stopper came out and solvent spilled over his genitals. He cleaned it off and checked the label on the bottle, which gave no information as to the danger to tender parts of the body or what remedial action to take. He later suffered extreme pain and had to have plastic surgery. Boots, as manufacturer and seller, was found liable, even though it had sold over 20 million such bottles with the same label and only received a handful of minor complaints. It knew the solvent could be dangerous, so should have redesigned the bottle to prevent spillage and/or given an effective warning. Damages were, however, reduced by 25% due to the plaintiff's contributory negligence.

A warning is not a substitute for a design fix

Because a warning can so easily be ignored or otherwise fail to prevent damage, the prime duty is to seek to 'engineer out' the hazard by design changes, additional safety devices or better production techniques. However, this has to be set against the customer's expectation of a realistic price and utility of the product. While it might be technically feasible to eliminate the hazard, the benefits of not doing so may outweigh the risk. In such cases the producer fulfils his legal duty by warning the user who then assumes the risk. This is particularly relevant when the producer offers different versions of the same basic model — the more expensive having additional safety features.

Obvious and non-obvious dangers

The producer is required to warn of the non-obvious dangers associated with the product, arising both from its intended use and foreseeable misuse.

For example, it is obvious that to drive a car with a flat tyre could lead to an accident; however, if a car capable of travelling at 100 m.p.h. is fitted with tyres whose maximum safe operating speed is only 85 m.p.h. then liability could arise either for a design defect or for failure to warn.[10] This is so even though it is illegal to drive at 100 m.p.h., or if the driver is drunk. The driver might be prosecuted for committing a criminal offence, but the civil liability of the producer still arises because it is foreseeable that if the vehicle is capable of 100 m.p.h. then it will be driven at such speeds. In such cases there may be contributory negligence by the victim.

When a danger is obvious there is no need to warn against it.[11] The duty arises from the presumption of unequal knowledge — where the producer or supplier has, or should have, a greater knowledge of the hazards than the user.

How much knowledge can be assumed of the user?

That depends on the foreseeability test: if laymen are likely to be exposed then the level of information given must be appropriate for such unqualified, inexperienced persons for whom the danger or its seriousness may not be obvious. If the product has only professional or experienced users, then a higher level of knowledge can be assumed.

Some American courts have taken this principle to ridiculous extremes. For example, in one case[12] a householder put his hand through the broken window of an electricity meter box to remove pieces of the glass and suffered an electric shock. The box had no warning on it regarding the danger of shock, or instructions that the supply should be disconnected. The Illinois court decided that a person with such intelligence and experience as the plaintiff might reasonably expect that a meter box in his backyard would be properly insulated and designed to prevent shock, i.e., the danger was not sufficiently obvious, so a warning should have been given.

In contrast, an experienced electrician, who was burned when he opened the door of a control box and touched live wires attached to a relay switch, failed in an action against the manufacturer. The court held:

(a) The manufacturer has a duty to warn the user of *any unusual danger* involved with the use of the product.

(b) The warning must adequately inform the user of any unusually dangerous propensities about which the manufacturer knows or should have known. The manufacturer is held to the degree of knowledge and skill of experts. The duty to warn will be imposed when there is unequal knowledge, actual or constructive, and where the manufacturer, possessed of such knowledge, knows or should know that harm might occur if no warning is given.

(c) There is no duty to warn when the manufacturer and user have equal knowledge of the danger.

In this case[13] the plaintiff alleged there were inadequate instructions on how to assemble the relay switch, replace parts, or incorporate it into a circuit; inadequate warnings that only properly insulated wires and parts should be used, and no warning to indicate its dangerous properties.

The court found that the switch was not substantially different to any other switch the plaintiff had used in his work and therefore no more dangerous; that he had several years' experience and some academic schooling in electrical work, and therefore was familiar with both the switch and its dangers.

A producer can take advantage of this ruling by positively limiting the marketing of his products to professionals, e.g., through 'trade only' outlets. With certain products this may seem unnecessary, e.g., high-technology machinery will only be used by trained operators. Nevertheless, the producer should ensure that this is the case by specifying what degree of training is required.

What about misuse and downright stupidity?

Examples abound of people trying to do crazy things with products, injuring themselves and then saying they were not warned of the danger:

● cutting a hedge with a rotary lawn mower;

● pouring flammable cologne perfume on a lighted candle to give it a scent;

● allowing children to play near the open mouth of an auger feeder (a powered rotating shaft) on a farm;

● freeing straw by putting a hand into a jammed baler without first switching off the power;

● drinking fluid from a car battery;

● stopping a lawn mower by jamming a foot in the blades.

● and, of course, the legendary poodle which the lady shampooed and put in the microwave oven to dry;

to which the reaction might be: 'Only an idiot would do that; why should the producer be liable?'

While these examples may be extreme, and not all of them rendered the producer liable (even in America!), it is well known that the majority of accidents are caused by human error, and not all victims are idiots. They are average human beings who, like everyone else, have limited knowledge and occasionally take chances. To them the risk was not sufficiently obvious or serious enough to deter them from taking it. Misuse, ignorance and risk-taking are foreseeable, and if a warning can provide an effective deterrent then the producer is expected to give it.

So, in *Moran v Fabergé Inc.*[14] the manufacturer of cologne perfume was found liable when a teenage girl was burnt after her friend poured some of it on to a lighted candle. There should have been a warning that the cologne was flammable.

The problem for the producer is therefore twofold:

(a)   How to predict the possible misuse.

(b)   How to ensure the warning is adequate.

Predicting misuse requires more than a vivid imagination. Ideally pre-launch tests should be carried out, using samples of suitably inexperienced and ignorant potential users, noting their reaction to different forms of warning and asking for suggested improvements. Once marketed it is a matter of responding to actual misuse: a producer may not have predicted that anyone would drink fluid from a car battery; once it happens it then becomes foreseeable and the expectation grows that a warning should be given to prevent recurrence.

To be adequate the warning should:

●   identify the seriousness of the risk;

●   describe the nature of the risk so that the user will understand it;

●   have the intensity to motivate the user to react;

●   provide information on how to avoid the hazard;

●   be conspicuous;

●   be permanent or easily replaceable during service;

●   reach the ultimate user;

●   indicate the consequences of ignoring the warning if these are not obvious.

For example, suppose an aerosol paint spray gives off vapours which are both highly flammable and can cause eye irritation. A warning: 'Danger — Harmful Vapours' might be held inadequate because it does not explain:

(a)   the precise nature of the risk (poisonous, flammable, eye irritant);

(b)   how to avoid it (use only in a well-ventilated area; no naked flames; wear protective goggles; keep out of reach of children);

(c)   the possible consequences (may cause streaming of the eyes; highly flammable);

(d)   any remedial action (bathe eyes in clean water; use only carbon dioxide fire extinguishers).

Accompanying symbols will reinforce the message and convey it to those who cannot (or will not) read.

Some producers seem to think that potential customers will be scared off by warnings. The sales and the reputation of the product may suffer, so they omit or understate the hazards. Writers of user manuals sometimes see their role as promoting the good features rather than pointing out the dangers.

The result can be a polite suggestion that there may be some minor inconvenience for the user, which he need not really worry about. The lost sales theory is probably fallacious: people are aware that certain products are dangerous, yet quite prepared to use them provided the risks are fully explained. In any case what are a few lost sales compared to a lost product liability case?

The warning message should have a 'cutting edge' which motivates the user to react. A terse: 'Incorrect operation can cause severe or fatal injury. Read instructions before use', is a better motivator than: 'Please read instructions before use'.

The user may be faced with pages of instructions. It is foreseeable that he may not bother to read them all, so the producer should take steps to persuade him.

Stating the consequences of ignoring the warning is the best motivator, since a natural reaction when faced with warnings is: 'Why should I take any notice?' A good example is the case of the Virginian farmer who sprayed his apple orchard and then sued the manufacturer because no leaves appeared on the trees for the next three years. Of course the spray packs had on them in big red letters: 'Do not spray after the first leaves appear', and, of course, the farmer ignored that warning. The American court found the warning inadequate because it did not also state something to the effect: 'If you spray after the first leaves appear, you will not have any leaves for the next three years'.

However, in a recent English case[15] it has been held that the manufacturer need not point out the *precise* nature of the consequences, provided a general warning is given. A farmer had purchased a weed-killer specifically to kill off wild oats growing in his crop of winter wheat. The packaging contained precise instructions about how and when to apply it, with a warning:

> 'Do not apply to wheat or barley crops beyond the recommended crop growth stage. Damage may occur to crops sprayed after the recommended growth stage. Damage may result unless all recommendations are followed.'

The farmer delayed spraying due to weather conditions, but thought the risk of late application was confined to damage to the growing crop — a risk he was prepared to take to clear the wild oats. In fact late application meant the weed-killer was ineffective against the wild oats, because they had developed too far.

The Court of Appeal decided (reversing the High Court judgment) that having given clear instructions and a warning that damage could result from late application, the manufacturer was not required to explain why those directions were given or how the weed-killer worked.

It would seem here that the manufacturer had just about managed to provide an adequate warning in the circumstances, but this was a case brought under the Sale of Goods Act 1979, s. 14, to decide whether the nature of the warnings rendered the goods unmerchantable or unfit for the particular purpose. The damage was purely financial, in that the farmer had wasted time and money on an ineffective weed-killer. A court might come to a different decision if the risk were safety-related and the claim brought under CPA 1987.

The warning should be conspicuous to those at risk

If a warning is too small, hard to locate, liable to be covered in dirt, peel off etc., then the argument: 'We put the warning on — it's up to the user to read it" may not hold up.

Where should the warning be put?

The simple answer is where it will be seen before or when using the product. Ideally the message should be attached permanently to the product, but that is not always possible with limited space and means of fixing. With complex products one cannot put on a label every warning or instruction that might appear in a well-drafted manual. An acceptable compromise is to place one or more general warnings on the product itself referring the user to the detailed manual.[16] While courts have accepted this method, it should not be taken as a licence to get away with fewer warnings. An effective balance has to be struck between the number and seriousness of the hazards, available space and feasibility, as part of the whole 'package' of information presented to the user.

This brings us back to the 'consumer expectation test'. The consumer expects to be warned in a manner reflected by current standards. One producer's warnings will be compared with another's, with the state of technology, level of risk, likely usage and all other relevant factors.

Is it enough to put a warning just in a manual?

Only if the producer can convince a court that it is the most effective place to get the message across. If he is aware that many users do not in practice have access to the manual, either because it is not attached or stored with the product, or because a first buyer does not hand it on to a subsequent buyer, or for any other reason, then could he reasonably be expected to do more to communicate the warning?

Warning lights or alarms are particularly conspicuous, but many are arguably unnecessary if the user follows the warnings and instructions in the manual. Should a car manufacturer, for example, be expected to incorporate a 'Parking brake on' or 'Fit seat belt' warning light or buzzer on the dashboard?

In *Kay* v *Cessna Aircraft Co.*[17] an aircraft with front and rear engines crashed during take-off. The rear engine had stopped as the pilot taxied to the runway, and he tried to take off without realising that only the forward engine was operating. The allegation was that Cessna should have put a warning light in the cockpit to alert the pilot to the fact that the rear engine was not running. Cessna argued that the manual spells out all procedures and instrument checks to carry out before take-off which, if done, alert the pilot. The plaintiff further alleged that even if those instructions were adequate, the possibility that a pilot would fail to comply fully with them was a foreseeable misuse of the aircraft.

The California jury found for the plaintiff, but on appeal the decision was reversed. The instructions were adequate, the pilot's failure to check his instruments was not reasonably foreseeable, Cessna could not be expected to have anticipated such misuse and therefore was not liable.

A different decision was reached in another American case involving instructions in a car handbook. The danger was heat from a catalytic converter on the exhaust system of the car which, if parked on long dry grass, could cause the grass to ignite. The handbook explained the danger, the driver duly failed to read it, parked on dry grass, and fell asleep. He woke with his car in flames. The court found that the handbook warning was inadequate, on the basis that it is well-known that many car drivers do not read lengthy handbooks, nor can be expected to do so. The warning could have been on the car, for example, on the sun-visor or dashboard, or alternatively the hazard designed out by better shielding. Other manufacturers had done this, so the consumer could expect better protection.

Surely a producer should not be liable if the user fails to read or disregards a clear warning?

The legal answer is: not necessarily. The question is not so much: How did the user fail? rather: How did the producer fail? Could the producer foresee that the warning would be ignored, and if so could he reasonably be expected to do something about it?

Under English Law and that of most jurisdictions the principles of contributory negligence and voluntary assumption of the risk will apply where some degree of fault lies with the user, i.e., the court reduces the damages as it thinks just and equitable having regard to the claimant's share in responsibility for the damage.

How much fault can be attributed to a user for not reading, understanding, remembering or observing a warning? Often 100%. If it is obvious that a hazard exists and there are clear warnings, e.g., wiring instructions on electrical goods, assembly instructions on goods supplied in kit form, then the user can hardly complain if he fails to observe them. However, he may get some damages where a product has hazards unusual in that type of product; or where its specification has recently been changed to present a fresh hazard; or he performs some routine operation which he normally would assume is safe.

What can be expected of a user in these circumstances? To read, understand and remember the whole of a complicated book of instructions? Often the supplier does not expect him to do so, e.g., when hiring or test-driving a car the handbook may be in the glove compartment, but the customer would not be expected to spend an hour reading it before driving off: at most a perfunctory glance to work out the major controls. It could be argued that the customer has 'constructive' notice, but the courts may not always favour that argument, particularly where the circumstances show no genuine expectation or opportunity for him to see the warnings. So, if an unusual hazard exists the warning may need to be more conspicuously placed.

What if the user is illiterate or does not speak the language in which the warning is written?

An English judge once said: 'Illiteracy is not a privilege'. A producer can at least assume that people in England can read English, and not have to put the warning in other languages for the benefit of foreign visitors. If exporting to a specific country, then it is reasonable to expect that country's language.

The difficulty arises when the product is likely to be sold or to circulate in a number of countries, or in a country with more than one language. For a product likely to be sold throughout Europe it might be reasonable to expect at least the user manuals and instruction leaflets in the major languages. In an American case[18] two Puerto Rican workers died after coming into contact with chemicals used for crop spraying. The label, in English, warned that protective clothing and a mask should be worn. The manufacturer was found liable because it was foreseeable that the product might be used by persons whose English or reading ability was limited.

For the warning actually affixed to the product the problem is lack of space for all those languages. A prominent symbol may be more conspicuous and effective than small print in six languages. Provided that warning, whether in words or symbols, effectively alerts the user to a danger, he can then be expected to refer to the manual or leaflets for further information.

The child warning

Another group of people at risk through inability to read or understand warnings are young children, who also have an amazing propensity to misuse things.

In one case[19] a toddler found a tin of floor polish, known by the manufacturer to contain poison, and proceeded to eat some. It was held that the manufacturer should have predicted this and was liable for not marking the contents as poison to warn parents to keep the tin out of reach of children. He could also have put a childproof top on the tin.

In another case[20] a 12 year-old boy was caught in the blades of an auger feeder and had his leg amputated from the knee down. He had been playing with other children around the machine and attempted to step over the unguarded auger. Advertising material for the machine stated: 'Even a child can do your feeding'. The court found the machine was unreasonably dangerous without an auger cover, that it was foreseeable that a child would be near it and could get caught. The danger was not so obvious that a warning could be omitted. Even though a child might not heed it, an adult would be alerted to take steps to protect children.

Where there is more than one producer or supplier, who should be responsible for issuing the warning?

The simple answer is that all those who could be held liable for a defect should ensure the adequacy of warnings. In practice those further down the manufacturing and distribution chain often simply pass on warnings given to them by their suppliers, without bothering to check. With strict liability this will not enable them to escape liability to a victim if the warning is defective, though they may have a defence to a criminal charge.

However, it is not always possible or necessary for each person in the chain to issue full warnings, e.g., a manufacturer of parts that have numerous applications cannot be expected to issue fitting instructions for all possible applications. Even if he knows the particular usage he will probably have done enough by stating; 'Refer to original equipment manufacturer's fitting instructions'.

The legal test is the same: could the consumer expect anything more? Do other producers give fuller warnings?

Can the duty to warn be delegated?

Sometimes a manufacturer relies on an intermediary, such as a dealer, employer or installer to convey warnings to the ultimate user. If that is not done effectively, can the manufacturer escape liability?

Generally the duty to warn is non-delegable. It is the manufacturer's responsibility to decide what warnings should be given and to ensure they reach the people at risk. However, in limited circumstances it may be sufficient to warn a professional intermediary, e.g., with prescribed drugs it is enough to warn doctors of possible side effects, reactions etc., without placing a similar warning on the pack given to the patient. Thereafter it is up to the doctor to decide what warnings he gives, taking all circumstances into account including the patient's understanding and wishes at the time. Schoolteachers have been recognised as responsible intermediaries in deciding what to tell children and parents about the dangers of products used in school. A manufacturer of hair dye, which he knew could be dangerous to certain skins, was found to have done enough by putting a warning on the packs supplied to hairdressers.[21] Any responsibility for warning customers then lay with the hairdresser.

Otherwise the manufacturer will bear some or all of the liability. To say to a retailer, 'Remember to tell customers about this danger' would be insufficient: it is foreseeable that the retailer will not, either because he forgets or because he is worried about losing a sale. Similarly it is insufficient to give an employer an operator's manual and tell him to pass it on to the employees who will actually use the product: it is foreseeable that that will not happen because the employer might want to keep the manual clean and safe for a future resale; he may think his employees already know enough about the product etc. In such circumstances the manufacturer could be expected to do more, e.g., attaching the warning or manual to the product, making multiple copies available, giving out copies during training sessions. Certainly he should alert users to the importance of reading the manual by attaching a general warning to each product supplied.

The post-sale duty to warn

To what extent does a producer have a duty to warn of dangers subsequently discovered in the product? He can be compelled by a notice to warn issued under CPA 1987, but that will only arise when the enforcement authorities, with their limited resources, become aware of the situation and are minded to take action.

(The possibility of recalls and retrofits also arises. This will be discussed in chapter 8.)

Two basic situations can be identified:

(a)   The defect was originally there, but the producer only subsequently became aware of it, e.g., contaminated ingredients, poor welds.

Here the product was defective when put into circulation. Logically under a strict liability system the producer would be liable for any resulting damage or injuries no matter how much effort he put into a subsequent warning or recall campaign. That harsh approach has not generally been adopted in the USA, where it has been held that the producer's obligation is fulfilled by taking all reasonable steps to warn, i.e., negligence principles apply. Previous cases in England have been based on negligence and it is not yet clear how CPA 1987 will be applied. In one case[22] employees alleged they had contracted cancer of the bladder as a result of being exposed during their employment to a chemical, Nonox S, containing carcinogenic substances. The defendant manufacturer argued that the dangers were not fully realised when that chemical was first developed, only becoming apparent later. The duty was stated as follows:

> Thus, if, when a product is first marketed, there is no reason to suppose that it is carcinogenic, but thereafter information shows, or gives reason to suspect, that it may be carcinogenic, the manufacturer has failed in his duty if he has failed to do whatever may have been reasonable in the circumstances in keeping up to date with knowledge of such developments and acting with whatever promptness fairly reflects the nature of the information and the seriousness of the possible consequences.

> If the manufacturer discovers that the product is unsafe, or has reason to suspect that it may be unsafe, his duty may be to cease forthwith to manufacture or supply the product in its unsafe form . . . giving proper warning to persons to whom the product is supplied of the relevant facts, as known or suspected, giving rise to the actual or potential risk.

The Health and Safety at Work etc Act 1974, s. 6 has now been amended by CPA 1987 to put this duty on a statutory basis, with the possibility of prosecution for breach. Any person who designs, manufactures, imports or supplies any article for use at work or any article of fairground equipment has to provide safety information and *revisions* of information as risks become known.[23]

It is established that if the user does in fact acquire knowledge of the danger, then he cannot recover for any subsequent loss which he ought to have avoided by taking remedial or precautionary steps. It is as if the warning was always there. The problem is proving that the warning message reached him.

(b)   The product met safety standards when made, but subsequent technical advances now provide improved safety, e.g., the new model has a safety device not fitted on the old; the danger has only recently been discovered (as with products containing asbestos).

The old model was not 'defective', given that it met the consumer expectations at the time. CPA 1987 specifically states that a defect shall not be inferred from the fact alone that the safety of a product which is supplied later is greater than the safety of the product in question.[24] Clearly it would be totally unreasonable to require a producer to recall and modify all previous models every time he launches an improved safety feature. That would involve constant recall campaigns and deter innovation.

Should he at least put out a warning about the dangers of the old, inform users of the new feature, or make it available as a 'bolt-on' addition if that is feasible?

Few court cases have arisen on this point. Sometimes with a newly discovered danger, such as side effects from drugs or metal fatigue in aircraft, a government authority will be involved in a warnings or recall campaign. The producer will be required to work closely with that authority in providing information, withdrawing existing stocks, tracing users and establishing a rectification system. However, for the majority of products it is left to the manufacturer to decide whether he should take any action, and the courts have disagreed about whether any liability can arise for failure to do so.

A New Jersey court in 1979 flatly denied that a manufacturer has 'any duty to monitor changes in technology and notions of safety and, either periodically or otherwise, notify its purchasers thereof'. In that case[25] the plaintiff had been injured while using a machine built and installed in 1931, some 42 years before the accident. Since then the industry had developed 'new, updated or improved safeguards desirable or required' for that type of machinery, but the manufacturer had not informed customers (including the plaintiff's employer) about these. The court said that this failure did not violate any duty. Evidence did not show that in 1931 the machine suffered from a design, manufacturing or warnings defect:

> There is no duty upon the seller of a machine faultlessly designed and manufactured . . . to notify its customers after the time of sale of changes in the state of the art concerning the safe operation of such machine and advise them to install any new, updated or improved safeguards developed since the time of sale.

The court accepted that cases from other jurisdictions mentioned a 'continuing duty to warn'. But these all involved defects existing, though unknown, at the time of sale. Any continuing post-sale duty to warn in such cases merely recognised that a duty existed at the time of sale. Where, as here, the product was free from any defects when sold, there was no initial duty to warn and so no duty can be said to 'continue'.

Other courts in the USA have applied a theory that with the benefit of hindsight the product was originally 'unreasonably dangerous',[26] therefore a duty to warn could be said to exist at the time and so continue. Thus as soon as the producer actually becomes aware of the danger he should issue a warning.

The Wisconsin Supreme Court discussed this theory in 1979 in a case[27] where a man was killed at work while cleaning a sausage stuffing machine. Pressure on a piston caused it to move beyond its normal position, fracturing nearby ammonia pipes and causing asphyxiation. Since the machine had been installed the manufacturer had developed a safety valve which would have prevented such an accident. It advertised the valve in trade publications, listed it as a safety attachment in a catalogue, and made it standard equipment on later machines. However, it did not notify the man's employer by any direct means, and representatives who had visited the premises made no mention of the new safety valve. The court held on this evidence that the manufacturer had violated a duty, either under a negligence or a strict liability theory. However, it immediately limited that duty:

We do not in this decision hold that there is an absolute continuing duty, year after year, for all manufacturers to warn of a new safety device which eliminates potential hazards. A sausage stuffer and the nature of that industry bears no similarity to the realities of manufacturing and marketing household goods such as fans, snow-blowers or lawn mowers which have become increasingly hazard proof with each succeeding model. It is beyond reason and good judgment to hold a manufacturer responsible for a duty of annually warning of safety hazards on household items, mass produced and used in every American home, when the product is 6 to 35 years old and outdated by some 20 newer models equipped with every imaginable safety innovation known in the state of the art. It would place an unreasonable duty upon these manufacturers if they were required to trace the ownership of each unit sold and warn annually of new safety improvements over a 35-year period.

As noted, the sausage stuffer machine industry is far more limited in scope. Consequently, a jury in determining a manufacturer's duty in this restricted area must look to the nature of the industry, warnings given, the intended life of the machine, safety improvements, the number of units sold and reasonable marketing practices, combined with the consumer expectations inherent therein.

Faced with this unclear legal position, what in practice can the producer do to minimise his potential liability?

- Instruct used equipment dealers to point out the lack of the safety feature on old models when offering them for sale or hire.

- Make available the new device as a 'bolt-on' option (if feasible) which can be purchased, together with full installation instructions and any technical assistance required.

- Make such availability a prominent feature in spares catalogues, service manuals etc.

- In any contact with users, e.g., servicing, operator training, new sales promotions, point out the danger and suggest an upgrading or replacement of the old product.

- Do not suggest that the original design was defective when sold, merely that technical advances now provide for improved safety.

Once a warning has been given, need it be repeated?

The duty to warn continues during the foreseeable life of the product. Under CPA 1987, a producer can only be strictly liable for up to 10 years from the time of supply, but beyond that period liability could still arise for negligence.

Whether a warning needs to be repeated depends on factors such as the durability of the original warning; the likelihood of defacement, dirt, paint, weathering etc. rendering it inconspicuous, and of resale without accompanying manuals, labels or leaflets; the turnover of operators or users who may not have seen the original warning.

For example, with a piece of industrial equipment with a 10-year life span, if all operators in year one are issued with a set of warnings how many operators in year seven will have seen them? With a 10% a year turnover only some 30%. Should it be expected that the employer or the original operators will pass on the message? It would surely be more reasonable to expect the manufacturer or supplier to repeat the warnings for the benefit of the 70% at risk? He should have a system for repeating and reinforcing, such as:

- Replacement decals, labels, manuals etc. available for users and distributors. A charge can be made.

●   Checks during service that the warnings are in place.

●   Training and demonstration sessions that emphasise the dangers as well as the method of operation.

●   Responding to feedback that warnings are being detached or otherwise failing to reach users.

How should subsequent warnings be communicated?

Beyond the prescription of any 'notice to warn' issued by the authorities, it is again a matter of 'taking reasonably practical steps'.

What other producers have done in similar circumstances is a useful pointer.

The duty, to the extent that it exists, is owed to users, not merely to distributors or even to purchasers.

In *Walton* v *British Leyland UK Ltd,*[28] severe injuries occurred when a rear wheel came off an Allegro car travelling at 50–60 m.p.h. on a motorway. The cause was hub bearing failure due to overtightening. BL had introduced tapered bearings on a number of its models, which required 'end-float', i.e., less tightness than on the flat bearings of previous models. There was nothing defective about the bearing itself, made by a reputable manufacturer and in use on thousands of cars throughout the world. No blame was attached to that manufacturer or to BL for using it. However, BL became aware that through unfamiliarity and disregard of instructions by service mechanics, overtightening was occurring. Over 100 reports of 'wheel adrift' had been received.

BL responded with a design change incorporating a larger washer to improve bearing security, and issued service bulletins to its franchised dealers and certain others only, at first emphasising the importance of 'end-float' and later instructing them to fit the larger washers when servicing brakes or hubs of earlier cars.

This campaign was held to be 'totally inadequate', because:

> . . . outside this limited safety net were left, in ignorance of the risk to which Leyland knew they were subject, a very large number of Allegro owners.

The duty owed by BL was:

> ... to make a clean breast of the problem and recall all the cars which they could in order that the safety washers could be fitted.

There was:

> ... a failure to observe their duty of care for the safety of the many who were bound to remain at risk, irrespective of the recommendations made to Leyland dealers and to them alone.

The duty can be fulfilled by trying to contact all users at risk. If they are known or their identity can be discovered, then direct mail or personal contact can be made. If using letters, then recorded delivery is advisable, obtaining a positive acknowledgement to refute any future claim that the message was not received. If that only elicits a partial response then a follow-up is needed, using progressively more direct means of communication. If users are not known, as with the majority of consumer goods bought in shops, then a media campaign is a reasonable expectation. Its intensity will depend on the level of risk, numbers exposed etc. compared to the cost and practicality of the campaign. The assistance of trade associations, consumer organisations, safety authorities (e.g., Trading Standards Department), insurance companies and others with vested interests can be enlisted, though they have no duty themselves and cannot have any delegated to them.

SUMMARY

Avoiding the creation of defects obviously involves having good standards, procedures and resources. It is also a matter of awareness and attitude: if staff are aware of what the law demands and think in terms of possible product liability implications, then many unnecessary defects can be avoided.

NOTES

1   *Dreisonstok v Volkswagenwerk AG* (1974) 489 F 2d 1066 (4th Circuit).

2   *Turner v General Motors Corporation* (1974) 514 SW 2d 497 (Texas)

3   *Larsen v General Motors Corporation* (1968) 391 F 2d 495 (8th Circuit).

4   *Bernier v Boston Edison Co.* (1980) 403 NE 2d 391 (Massachusetts).

5   See H. Abbott, *Safer by Design: The Management of Product Design Risks under Strict Liability* (London: Design Council, 1987).

6   *Wormell v RHM Agriculture (East) Ltd* [1987] 1 WLR 1091; *Vacwell Engineering Co. Ltd v BDH Chemicals Ltd* [1971] 1 QB 88.

7   Medicines Act 1968.

8   Food Act 1984 and subordinate regulations.

9   (1962) 106 SJ 552.

10   *LeBouef v Goodyear Tire & Rubber Co.* (1978) 451 F Supp 253 (WD Louisiana).

11   *Crow v Barford (Agricultural) Ltd and H.B. Holttum & Co. Ltd* Court of Appeal 8 April 1963.

12   *Troszynski v Commonwealth Edison Co.* (1976) 356 NE 2d 926 (Illinois).

13   *Peterson v B/W Controls Inc.* (1977) 366 NE 2d 144 (Illinois).

14   (1975) 332 A 2d 11 (Maryland).

15   *Wormell v RHM Agriculture (East) Ltd* [1987] 1 WLR 1091

16   Two American examples illustrate the problem: *Scott v Black & Decker Inc.* (1983) 717 F 2d 251 (5th Circuit): 'To require that one explicit warning be placed on the [electric] saw would be to require all twenty'. *Broussard v Continental Oil Co.* (1983) 433 So 2d 354 (Louisiana): 'In view of the numerous risks which a manufacturer of a hand drill must explicitly describe, . . . the most practical and effective thing which the manufacturer could do is to direct the user to the owner's manual'.

17   (1977) 548 F 2d 1370 (9th Circuit).

18   *Hubbard-Hall Chemical Co.* v *Silverman* (1965) 340 F 2d 402 (1st Circuit).

19   *Spruill* v *Boyle-Midway Inc.* (1962) 308 F 2d 79 (4th Circuit).

20   *DeSantis* v *Parker Feeders Inc.* (1976) 547 F 2d 357 (7th Circuit).

21   *Holmes* v *Ashford* [1950] 2 All ER 76.

22   *Wright* v *Dunlop Rubber Co. Ltd* (1972) 13 KIR 255.

23   Health and Safety at Work etc. Act 1974, s. 6 as amended by Consumer Protection Act 1987, sch. 3. See also chapter 5.

24   Consumer Protection Act 1987, s. 3(2).

25   *Jackson* v *New Jersey Manufacturers Insurance Co.* (1979) 400 A 2d 81 (New Jersey).

26   For example, *Beshada* v *Johns-Manville Products Corporation* (1982) 447 A 2d 539 (New Jersey), where the court imputed the manufacturer with knowledge of the product's dangers (long-term exposure to asbestos) notwithstanding that at the time of the product's marketing these dangers were undiscoverable given the existing state of scientific knowledge. But in *Feldman* v *Lederle Laboratories* (1984) 479 A 2d 374 (New Jersey) the same court later limited this to imputing to the manufacturer the knowledge which was 'reasonably knowable' at the time.

27   *Kozlowski* v *John E. Smith's Sons Co.* (1979) 275 NW 2d 915 (Wisconsin).

28   Judgment of 12 July 1978, Queen's Bench Divisional Court, set out in C.J. Miller and G.W. Harvey, *Consumer and Trading Law — Cases and Materials* (London: Butterworths, 1985).

7

Incriminating Evidence

The victim of an allegedly defective product may bring a civil action against those he considers responsible. In England this will be in a county court or in the High Court, depending on the type of action and size of the claim.

The detailed procedure for issuing writs, defences, counter-claims etc. need not concern us.[1] The part of the process with implications for managing product liability exposure is the access the plaintiff has to information.

In building up his case before it comes to trial the plaintiff (i.e., his lawyers) will wish to obtain as much information as possible, hopefully incriminating, from the defendant producer or supplier. While under strict liability principles it is not necessary to prove that the defendant was aware of the risk, or had failed to take reasonable care to prevent it, if such evidence can be found then it becomes easier to show that the product was defective at the time of supply. Additionally if the case is brought on the basis of negligence or, in the USA, if punitive damages are sought, then such evidence is essential.

The defendant will no doubt wish to withhold such evidence, at least until the trial itself. Perhaps a pre-trial settlement can meanwhile be negotiated, or the plaintiff otherwise decides to drop the case.

The legal procedure provides two main ways for getting information during the pre-trial period:

(a)   Discovery.

(b)   Interrogatories.

In the USA and certain other countries a third process is the deposition of witnesses.

DISCOVERY

Discovery is a requirement for disclosure of documents and other forms of record. Generally discovery is automatic: the parties disclose the list of documents within 14 days of the close of pleadings. Otherwise it can be ordered.[2]

Discovery applies to 'documents which are or have been in the possession, custody or power' of the party, and 'relating to any matter in question between them'. This means any document 'which, it is reasonable to suppose, contains any information which *may* . . . enable the party [applying for discovery] either to advance his own case or to damage the case of his adversary. . . . if it is a document which may fairly lead him to a train of inquiry, which may have either of these two consequences'.[3]

Providing the plaintiff sets out the general nature of his allegations and can establish that information in documents might be material to the claim, then he is entitled to disclosure of those documents. Thus in a claim by an employee injured due to allegedly defective brakes on a fork-lift truck, the maintenance reports showing previous repairs following complaints were clearly relevant:

> One of the objects [of discovery] is to enable the plaintiff to find out before he starts proceedings whether he has a good cause of action or not. That object would be defeated if he had to show in advance that he already had a good cause of action before he saw the documents. That reasoning applies to the present case. If the reports did show a want of proper maintenance or repair of this truck, an action would no doubt be brought. Whereas if they show that there was proper maintenance and repair, an action would not be brought.[4]

The term 'document' is not restricted to paper writings, but extends to 'anything upon which evidence or information is recorded in a manner to be intelligible to the senses or capable of being made intelligible by the use of equipment',[5] e.g., tape recordings, microfilms, computer-held information.

Discovery has two stages:

(a) Disclosure of what documents exist. A list of all documents relating to the matter must be produced, indicating those which the party has in his possession, those which he once had and who now has possession, and which (if any) he is not willing to disclose by claiming privilege. The list must state where and when the documents may be inspected.

(b) Inspection of documents. Through his lawyer the plaintiff inspects and if necessary copies those documents. This extends to using appropriate equipment. Where there are numerous complex documents it may be permissible for an independent expert to help sort through and interpret them, even though he is not a prospective witness.[6]

If a claim for privilege is made, the court can be asked to decide whether it is valid. Privilege is most commonly claimed on confidential communications between lawyer and client. However, it should not be thought that documents enjoy privilege simply by routing them via a solicitor, i.e., using him as a post-box for all sensitive communications. The referral to the lawyer must be a substantial, though not necessarily only, reason for drawing up the document.[7]

Privilege cannot be claimed simply by putting 'Confidential' or some similar term on a document.

If privileged documents do happen to fall into the hands of the other side, then an injunction can be sought to restrain their use.[8]

If the plaintiff thinks the list is incomplete he may make a further request and ask for verification by sworn affidavit. In extreme cases where there is a strong suspicion that the defendant is about to destroy or smuggle away documents the court may be asked to make an order permitting the applicant to enter and search his premises (an 'Anton Piller order'[9]).

Default in complying with the discovery process can result in the defence being struck out, costs awarded to the other side and the defaulter committed for contempt, i.e., both the company and the individual can be punished.

The general rule is that discovery is only available against a party to the proceedings, i.e., the defendant producer or supplier. Documents in the possession of non-parties can normally only be required to be brought to the trial itself, not inspected beforehand. However, a key exception to this rule is in personal injury or fatal accident cases. Thus test reports on the product done by other manufacturers would be obtainable.[10]

The safest assumption to make is that all relevant documents, wherever they are kept, are vulnerable to discovery.

What documents are likely to be subject to discovery?

In the typical product liability action a wide variety of documents may be required to be handed over, for example:

(a)   Test reports. What tests were carried out? By whom? What failures occurred? Were any modifications proposed and made, reservations expressed about the standard achieved and outstanding problems, recommendations made for further improvements? This need not be limited to the particular product at issue, but extend to other products in the producer's range and to any testing on similar products of other producers, seeking to establish what lessons might have been learnt.

(b)   Reports, analyses, memoranda, minutes, evaluations, costings etc., relating to design decisions. These could show whether alternative designs were considered, and if so why they were rejected. If a potentially safer design was feasible but not considered then the producer can be accused of not keeping up with latest technology and standards; if it was considered but rejected then he can be accused of putting cost, convenience or other commercial factors before safety.

(c)   Manufacturing, inspection and quality control records, including those of any component, ingredient or raw material supplier, and of subcontractors involved. These could establish the adequacy of manufacturing and testing processes, e.g., whether a sampling system could enable something to go through untested and with what degree of risk.

(d)   Documents on the service history of the product e.g., warranty claims; failures reported by customers or dealers;[11] accident reports;[12] what remedial action was taken to solve the problem. Here the evidence could reveal that the producer failed to take effective action when he became aware of the problem, e.g., merely making a design change for future production when a recall would have been appropriate.

Some requests name persons within the producer's organisation to disclose any documents they authored or have in their personal possession (even though it is the company being proceeded against rather than individual employees or agents[13]) e.g., if it is known that a particular engineer attended an outside conference on the safety matter involved in the case, then the conference papers may indicate his awareness of a safer design.

There are limits on what the plaintiff can require to be disclosed. The depth of discovery permitted by the English system is less than in America, and criticism has been made that this can prejudice the plaintiff's case. His application is through the court, not direct to the defendant, and the court then decides whether to issue the order for discovery as it thinks fit under the procedural rules.

As well as claiming privilege, the defendant may challenge the request for any document as being irrelevant, too broad, impossible or too burdensome to comply with. He may also refuse to yield documents which he considers will or might expose him to criminal proceedings. This would appear an excellent let-out, since with most allegedly defective products there might also be prosecution for failure to 'comply with the general safety requirement' under CPA 1987, Part II, or for breach of other safety regulations. In practice any criminal prosecution will have been disposed of before a civil action, and all such evidence will already have been revealed.

With documents containing technical secrets or other sensitive information the court will order a controlled measure of discovery to selected individuals on terms that there should be no further disclosure or use of the information.[14] The party obtaining discovery must not misuse documents for some other purpose than promoting the case.[15]

Challenges and fresh applications may be swapped, but ultimately the plaintiff is likely to gain a right of access to a wide range of recorded information, some of which may prove incriminating to the producer.

INTERROGATORIES

Interrogatories are written questions served (through the court) on a party to obtain further information relevant to the matter. This will help establish what is admitted and what is denied, thereby speeding up progress. Written answers are required, under oath, with meaningful detail. Again the defendant may challenge, commonly when he suspects the plaintiff is 'trawling' for information of general use with broad or irrelevant questions, or by claiming privilege. If the answers are thought insufficient, the plaintiff may serve further, usually more specific, questions. Default is dealt with in the same way as for discovery. Additionally any facts not disclosed in the answers may be barred in the subsequent trial, making it difficult to 'keep things up your sleeve'.

DEPOSITIONS

Depositions are a feature of the pre-trial process in certain jurisdictions, notably in the USA and Canada, which so far has been resisted in the UK. A producer will therefore only face this process in an action brought in such jurisdictions. For component producers this can arise if a finished product in which their component is included finds itself in such countries, even though it was manufactured and sold in the UK.

It involves an oral examination, under oath, for the purpose of obtaining facts relevant to the issue. A reporter is present to record everything said, and a transcript typed which is then available in any subsequent trial. Some depositions are also taped or video-recorded.

In the typical product liability case the plaintiff's lawyers will request the presence of a representative (deponent) for the defendant producer, who will be guided by his lawyers. The deponent will probably be a senior manager or engineer involved with the design or process at issue. The meeting usually takes place in a lawyer's premises, the proceedings are relatively informal with participants sitting down, allowed to smoke and drink coffee.

While the proper purpose is to obtain facts to facilitate the progress of the case by 'getting the cards on the table' before the trial itself, it must be remembered that the plaintiff's lawyer is not merely interested in facts but in winning the case. He will also be hoping to obtain punitive damages for his client. He will adopt a line of questioning to get admissions of carelessness, awareness of risks, cost taking priority over safety. He will ask for any opinions or reservations the deponent or others had or now have about the safety of the product, and with the benefit of hindsight what the producer could have done to reduce the danger. He will seek to discredit the producer in any way possible.

The deponent is therefore under considerable pressure, and must take care not to be led into giving too much away. He must of course tell the truth, but need not volunteer information in an effort to be helpful. If asked for an opinion he can truthfully respond: 'I don't have any opinion on this matter', rather than forming one on the spot. If not sure he should admit: 'I don't know' or 'I can't properly remember', and not make a guess. If then asked to guess or speculate he should refuse. It is often very difficult for a person who spends his working life trying to be helpful, making suggestions and not wishing to appear ignorant or forgetful to change his approach. With this in mind the deponent will invariably be given prior guidance and rehearsal with his lawyers. Some say the rehearsal is more harrowing than the actual deposition!

PROGRESS OF THE CASE TO TRIAL

The pre-trial disclosure of information may result in the case being dropped by the plaintiff through realisation that he will lose. Alternatively, the producer may offer a financial settlement, because he realises he has little defence and/or he does not wish to disclose information which could further damage his reputation through the publicity of a trial.

If the case does go to court then the discovery documents, answers to interrogatories and (in the USA and some other jurisdictions) deposition transcripts are available for comparison with statements from the witness box.

Once in court the more familiar process of questioning witnesses, receiving experts' reports and other admissible evidence will painstakingly grind to a conclusion. Subject to certain restrictions, this will be open to media reporting with the consequent effects on the defendant's reputation. Too often the allegations make the headlines; the fact that the producer successfully defends merits little attention.

WHAT ARE THEY LOOKING FOR? THE 'SMOKING GUN', THE 'UNEXPLODED BOMB' AND THE 'OPEN LOOP'

The plaintiff's lawyer will try everything within the bounds of the law to find and present evidence that is most damaging to the producer. Above all he is looking for the *smoking gun* — the evidence that proves, or can be made to appear to prove, that the defendant knew about the risk before the injury occurred and could have done something to prevent it. This can be in a variety of forms, but ideally a document such as an engineer's report recommending a safety improvement which was not then carried out.

When that document was written it immediately became an *unexploded bomb* in the hands of the defendant. Any report, memo, telex, minute or comment containing a safety-related proposal, opinion, problem, failure, weakness etc. can be regarded as such. Unless that bomb is somehow defused it presents a danger: ticking away in a file awaiting discovery.

Incriminating evidence would include:

- Design or testing programmes subject to unreasonable time or resource constraints, e.g., reports showing an inability to complete the work, with no satisfactory reaction by way of an extension of time or extra resources.

- Production targets forcing quality control processes to be skipped, e.g., manufacturing records showing that untested or non-approved parts were used; witnesses admitting that the predominant motive was to keep the production lines moving, with associated risk-taking.

- Lack of reaction to reports of failures and dangers, e.g., warranty claims or service reports not followed up by investigation into cause and necessary modification or rectification.

- A safety-related modification proposed but rejected on unjustifiable grounds, e.g., a reply from a finance function that the cost is too high. Then the lawyer can allege that the manufacturer recklessly put cost before safety.[16] Cost may be a legally acceptable reason for rejecting a proposal: the danger is when it dominates.

- Cost-reduction exercises which could prejudice safety, e.g., removing safety features from the product; lowering safety margins; switching from a proven component supplier to a cheaper one with lower standards.

- Failure to assess a potentially safer method, e.g., reports on a rival manufacturer's model, conference papers, trade journals etc., which show an awareness of the potential, but not followed by a proper assessment of whether it could be incorporated.

- Inadequate procedures for dealing with safety-related matters, e.g., no laid-down system for analysing complaints; no contingency plans for tracing and recalling defective products.

Worse still:

- Safety procedures not adhered to, e.g., inspection not done according to the stated procedure due to apathy, lack of time or resources, or employees devising a short-cut method. Nothing can be better for the lawyers than the admission: 'This is how we say the job should be done, but in practice we don't always do that'.

- Any form of admission that a problem exists, a failure has occurred, a modification is necessary, someone is at fault, standards are not high enough.

AVOIDING INCRIMINATING EVIDENCE IN WRITTEN COMMUNICATIONS AND DOCUMENTS

A common reaction on learning of the powers of discovery and the use by lawyers of the information is: 'I'll never write anything down again to do with safety'.

This reaction is naïve. The way to avoid liability is not simply to stop writing down any comments about the safety of the product. The problem does not cease to exist merely because it is not written down. Even if the defendant denies knowledge of the risk the lawyer can argue that he should have known about it.

The real issue is HOW the problem is stated and WHAT IS DONE about it, not refusing to admit its existence.

Let us consider four ways of tackling the problem of having incriminating evidence on documents and records:

(a)   Not writing the matter down in the first place.

(b)   Destroying all copies before they are discovered.

(c)   Ensuring that the evidence they contain is as harmless as possible.

(d)   Ensuring that if the document suggests that action can be taken to overcome the risk, then such action is taken and properly documented.

Unfortunately for the producer the first two ways are not as simple a solution as they might appear!

Not writing the matter down

This solution is not always possible, and anyway may not work. Complex or lengthy information cannot all be carried in one's head, nor properly analysed without being written down or recorded in some way. Even simple messages cannot always be communicated by personal or telephone contact. No business can function without committing some safety-related matters into writing.

Yet there are circumstances in which positive efforts could be made to avoid writing, even though that would be easier. The effort of calling a meeting, making a trip to see someone or having an expensive telephone call rather than simply sending a memo could pay off.

For example, suppose an engineer has a reservation about the safety of the design which proves to be unfounded, and suggests an alternative which proves to be unnecessary. He should discuss it first with his colleagues and have his fears allayed, rather than immediately raising a report. If he does write it down then he has planted the unexploded bomb, and the only safe way to defuse it is by a further report showing that the matter was discussed and the proper conclusion reached that no further action was necessary. The danger, of course, is that since no action is necessary no further report is thought necessary. Later the only record on file is a report of a potential problem and no indication of what was done about it. An *open loop* in the documentation, which the lawyer can exploit.

Writing is a two-edged weapon. When the lawyer asks: 'Did anyone consider an alternative design?' it is more helpful to answer: 'Yes. Here is an engineer's report where he suggested an alternative. We assessed it and here is the report showing it would not improve safety', rather than: 'I remember we discussed an alternative and rejected the idea' with no documented proof.

So what does that poor engineer do? If he can be sure that the matter he raises will result in action then he is helping his company's position by providing conclusive written evidence that proper consideration is given to possible alternative designs. If he is not so sure, then discussing the matter verbally only would seem safer.

This is not a very satisfactory basis on which to operate. Obviously if no document exists then the pre-trial discovery process will not reveal evidence of the suggested alternative design. But if the case proceeds to trial (or in a deposition) the lawyer will probably ask the question anyway, and the witness under oath and the pressure of examination will probably admit: 'Yes, an alternative was suggested'. The next questions: 'What action was taken?', and: 'Why is there no report on this? Doesn't your company have a procedure for raising and dealing with suggestions for design changes?'

So avoiding writing down the suggestion will not necessarily prevent the truth coming out, and the producer being in the embarrassing position of explaining the lack of documentation.

The proper solution for a responsible producer is to establish procedures which both encourage staff to report any perceived risks and ensure that they are dealt with so that *the loop is closed*. The system should flag any outstanding issues after set deadlines, raise their priority and insist on a conclusion. The engineer should then follow the procedure precisely, taking care *how* he expresses the issue (see below) but nevertheless accurately stating his perception of the risk, and then using all his influence to get appropriate action.

On to the next possible solution:

Destroying the written evidence

If the documents demanded look incriminating, why not deny they exist, destroy or alter them?

This is a natural reaction, and no doubt some defendants resort to it. But it is an extremely dangerous tactic and cannot be relied on for the following reasons:

(a) *Possible criminal offence.* Once a valid request for discovery has been made then default can lead to a criminal conviction: the defendant company, individuals within it and its solicitors could all face prosecution. Few employees are willing to risk that, and even fewer solicitors, no matter how loyal they are!

No offence is committed before a request is served, so the routine disposal of memoranda, reports etc. which clutter up a file is perfectly legal and probably essential to avoid being buried by a mountain of paper. Equally there is no obligation to commit things to writing in the first place, other than for securing necessary approval from certifying and standards bodies. However, if the relevant record does exist at the time then it must be listed and produced in compliance with the discovery rules.

(b) *Other copies.* So why not risk it? Who will know if the incriminating document has surreptitiously been destroyed? The plaintiff will surely then have less chance of proving anything?

Because there may be other copies, and not all of these are destroyed. The memo pointing out the hazard and recommending action which was never carried out might have had five names on the circulation list. Those five memos are retrieved and destroyed — but someone made a photocopy for another file and that one survives. If it is still within the company, then when found it could also be destroyed. But what if an ex-employee, supplier or other outsider has a copy? It has been known for disgruntled employees to deliberately keep copies of documents which otherwise have been destroyed and then offer these to a plaintiff's lawyer.

If someone was told to destroy a document, can you be sure he did so? Some people keep the most unlikely documents for years, which you assumed were consigned to the bin long ago. A document retention policy might state that after a certain number of years documents are to be destroyed, but were they? Other departments may have different retention policies.

(c) *The cross reference.* More difficult to detect is the apparently harmless document which contains a cross-reference to one that is clearly incriminating.

For example, a report on a test successfully carried out on one component which concludes by recommending that other components be given a similar test. One such component then fails this test, but no improvements are made. This failure report is destroyed because it looks incriminating, but the original report survives. When that report is later checked before being submitted to discovery it appears safe enough, but no one checked out the results of its recommendations. The smart lawyer then spots the recommendation and asks the obvious question: 'Were these other tests carried out?' To answer no begs the question: 'Why not?' To answer yes leads to: 'Where are the reports?'

So a policy of retaining the 'good' reports and destroying the 'bad' is likely to fail.

(d) *Other evidence reveals the content.* So what about destroying *all* documents, good and bad, and never retaining anything in writing again connected with safety? First because no business could run efficiently without maintaining documents. Secondly because if there is no recorded information the lawyers will call persons involved in the design, testing or manufacture etc. to the witness box and ask them what occurred.

'Did you carry out tests on this component?'

'Yes.'

'What were the results?'

'There were certain failures, such as . . .'

'Did you write a report on these failures and make any recommendations?'

'Yes.'

'Were these recommendations taken up?'

'No.'

'What happened to the report?'

'I don't know.'

Or, worse still: 'I was told to destroy it'.

The destruction of documents will not necessarily prevent the truth coming out, particularly when a witness is under oath and the pressures of cross-examination, during which he may reveal more damaging information that would be contained in a carefully written document.

(e) *A missing document assumes enormous importance.* A gap in the documentation will inevitably suggest it contained very damning evidence indeed, when it was actually only mildly incriminating. Better for the defendant to disclose the document and then try to explain and justify its contents than risk destroying it. If he is found to have withheld one piece of evidence, then what else might he be hiding? Can any of his evidence be relied on?

(f) *Evidence of destruction might lose the case.* If it is proved that a document was deliberately destroyed, withheld or altered, then as well as the possible criminal penalties the case itself will be significantly harder to defend and more costly. The defence may be struck out and a retrial ordered, in which case the producer will pay the costs. If judgment eventually goes against the producer then an award of exemplary damages is likely. Defending the case will be particularly difficult in those jurisdictions where a jury is present (e.g., USA). In America the reaction of a jury may not only result in the case being lost, but also an award of punitive damages.

So if that engineer with his reservation and suggestion adopts the attitude: 'I might as well write the thing down, and if nothing is done about it we can always destroy the documents later', then he treads a dangerous path.

Three conclusions can be drawn:

(a) Assume that anything written or recorded is subject to discovery.

(b) It will fall into the hands of the smart lawyer who will use it to his greatest advantage.

(c) Do not rely on destroying, withholding or altering the record later.

Staff must therefore be constantly aware that what they are writing is subject to discovery, and not assume that anything incriminating can simply be hidden. This awareness in itself can prevent much unnecessary incriminating evidence being created. For example, it is tempting in a report to exaggerate the seriousness of a safety hazard in order to make someone in the company take notice: with the awareness that one day a lawyer might see that report and use it against the company, then the originator might keep his comments more accurate and less self-damning.

A more sensible solution: ensuring that what is written down is as harmless as possible

The starting-point when writing anything is to assume that one day it will be discovered and used by a lawyer building up a case against you.

Writing about any safety-related issue should therefore always be done with more care and scrutiny than might be given to other issues. The costs of settling a product liability dispute are a reminder that such care is worthwhile.

This is largely the individual's responsibility: to be prepared to take more time and effort to get the facts right, give the correct emphasis, make valid conclusions etc. His colleagues and superiors should be willing to check and to suggest better ways of presenting the issue. Management can assist by offering guidance and providing a system for the vetting of sensitive communications, if necessary by legal staff or advisers. (Asking for such legal advice might be a matter of confidentiality for which privilege could be claimed on any subsequent discovery request.)

The following do's and don'ts suggest some ways of minimising the potential harm:

- *DO state facts.*

This is the first and most important do. It may be that by stating the facts the producer is incriminated, but by failing to state them the implications could be far worse!

Hiding the potentially damaging facts, lying or understating them can mean that no action follows to remedy the problem. If a case ever goes to court and the true facts are discovered then the producer is in an infinitely worse position: he would inevitably be found negligent, possibly reckless, and could face criminal as well as civil liabilities.

Accuracy is essential, first to enable others within the organisation to understand and respond and, secondly, to convince a court that proper care was taken to deal with the risk. The temptation to hide, understate or avoid mentioning the risk is great, but in the long term such a policy may prove counter-productive and extremely costly.

The responsible policy is to state the risk accurately: the causes, likelihood, consequences and possible solutions. Then get some action.

● *DO give full information to enable action to be taken.*

A shortage of accurate information can cause confusion, delay or failure in any action taken. The recipient may waste time and effort checking for information that could quite easily have been provided in the first place. The bomb that was set by the original communication remains ticking away. Meanwhile a defective product could be exposing the producer to legal claims not just on a strict liability basis but now also for negligence or recklessness. The lawyer who discovers that *something* was known about the risk will argue that here was sufficient awareness that the producer could have taken action to overcome it. He will not be convinced by the kind of argument: 'We couldn't take any action because our dealer didn't tell us the part number affected by this fault'.

Document design must encourage staff to give full information e.g., by providing appropriate headings, checklists, questions. Too often the format of a document restricts instead of encourages, with staff feeling obliged not to write beyond the space in the box provided. However, there is a danger that by providing too many blank spaces on a document, staff will be tempted to add opinions, irrelevant remarks and other possibly damaging comments. The document therefore should be carefully structured to ensure that all relevant facts can be fully reported and that any additional remarks are strictly related to those facts.

● *DON'T speculate.*

Guessing what *might* be the causes, consequences or solutions has the danger that what you intend as a vague possibility the lawyer interprets as a cast-iron certainty. He will argue that by your own admission the product was defective.

If there is no definite answer then the possibilities should be quantified by analysis, not pure speculation.

It is often difficult to avoid speculation. People wish to offer 'helpful' ideas, to point out the potential seriousness of the risk so that others react, and they feel morally obliged to state what might happen. Field personnel in particular face a problem: they are on the spot where the failure took place, but not always with the resources to analyse the cause or solution, yet are often expected to offer suggestions. If they do so their report must make absolutely clear that it is purely a suggestion based on limited information and expertise, and not a categoric statement of fact. This may mean a larger report, and where there is a premium on the number of words used, as in a telex or on a form with only a small space, the temptation is to cut out the qualifying words and stick to the bare essentials. So, instead of: 'Suggest you investigate the possibility of . . . as a solution', the message becomes: 'Solution is . . .'

When that report is received the suggestion must be investigated. If it is incorrect then a record must be kept showing why — to defuse the bomb. It is tempting to ignore what appears as a ridiculous idea from someone who does not know what he's talking about, but the lawyer will treat the idea as a correct one made by an expert, so there must be evidence to prove otherwise.

Similarly . . .

● *DON'T give unqualified opinions.*

Opinions are often sought or given, and decisions based on them. An engineer could be asked to test a new plastic component and compare it with the old metal version. His results show the plastic is not as strong but in his opinion safe enough for the intended use. That opinion is valid, coming from a qualified engineer. What he should not do is give his opinion on whether the cost savings of using plastic are worthwhile, or whether there will be lost sales because of customer resistance to cheap-looking materials, because he is not qualified in costing or marketing. Conversely the marketing expert can give a valid opinion on likely customer reaction, but should not comment on the safety aspects.

Giving opinions is very much part of human nature. Employees like to think they know everything about the product, that their opinion is valid and they are being helpful in giving it. Some like to show off their knowledge — it makes them feel important and might impress the boss.

Once any opinion about a safety-related risk has been expressed in writing then, as with any speculative comment, there needs to be evidence about what action was taken or why none was necessary.

● *DON'T exaggerate.*

Often a person will exaggerate the risk to try to get someone else to take notice. If that succeeds in getting appropriate action then all well and good. The danger is when it does not, because then a piece of evidence exists stating that here is a *serious* risk and nothing was done about it. Another 'own goal' stating that the product is defective. The producer then faces the prospect of having to discredit the originator.

Exaggeration is frequently resorted to on a second or subsequent communication. The first was entirely accurate but failed to get the desired response. The originator gets annoyed and repeats more forcibly what to him is an important issue: 'This is a serious safety hazard. If we don't do something about it immediately there will be hundreds of accidents.'

Persuading him not to exaggerate is difficult, because the end seems to justify the means. Maybe if he realised the use a lawyer could make of his reports and the potential costs of losing a case he might tone things down or find better arguments (such as improving sales) for prompting action.

● *DO be conservative in conclusions and remarks.*

The conclusions of a report or the remarks box on a form are often used as an opportunity to let off steam. The rest of the report is entirely factual, but here the writer can say what he really thinks. The exaggerations, speculations and unqualified opinions all come out. The facts do not suggest that the product is defective, the remarks do.

To the lawyer these remarks can be assumed to be as accurate as anything else on the report. How can the producer then argue that only part of the report should be believed?

● *DON'T imply that cost or resource constraints always take priority over safety.*

Cost may well be *one* reason for not improving, or actually lowering, safety levels. It is accepted that a producer has to make a saleable product, that customers are not prepared to pay for every conceivable safety improvement, that economic and other benefits can outweigh the risks involved. A car fuel tank might be safer if encased in armour-plate, the technology exists to do it, military vehicles may have it, but that is not a realistic proposition for the family runabout. The danger for the producer is indicating that cost is the *only* or the *dominant* reason.

So, if someone proposes armour-plate the answer should not be: 'No, you can't have it because it costs too much', but, after due consideration: 'It is not realistic to have it, given all the circumstances: the existing fuel tank is safe enough; it exceeds all mandatory and recommended standards, and is as safe as any other manufacturer's; armour-plate has many disadvantages (weight, effect on handling, fuel consumption etc.). It is also extremely costly and the customer would gain only a marginal improvement in safety, far outweighed by the disadvantages.'

Preferably omit any reference to cost.

In the minds of the producer's employees cost is usually such a constant pressure that it tends to obscure other reasons in written communications. Cost-reduction exercises can result in a lowering of safety levels in existing products. This may be justifiable where the existing product is over-engineered, unnecessarily strong, pure etc., so that there is no appreciable risk in changing it. Similarly, if other modifications make a safety feature superfluous, the product does not thereby necessarily become defective, but look at the documents detailing the modifications and what do we find? 'Reason for change: cost saving.'

A virtual admission by the producer that cost is the only factor, not the continued safety of the product. With a little effort the full reasons could have been stated, and the unnecessary implication that cost comes before safety avoided.

Resource constraints can equally lead to self-incrimination, e.g., 'We could improve the existing product but we're too busy working on the new one'. 'No resources can be spared to investigate any further proposals.'

What is probably intended by these statements is that purely cosmetic changes will not be considered. If a vital *safety* improvement becomes necessary then the resources will be found, so why imply otherwise?

●   *DON'T suggest that unreasonable risks are being taken.*

If you say: 'There is a risk that this could cause injury', the lawyer will argue: 'You admitted it was defective'.

Of course there are risks associated with virtually all products, some by their very nature (e.g., vehicles, chain-saws), others through misuse (e.g., solvents, medicines). Some manufacturing processes cannot be guaranteed infallible, even when using latest state-of-the-art technology. Arguably the very production of such things is an admission of risk-taking, but that does not necessarily create a legal liability. So when nothing more can be expected through redesign, improved manufacturing processes or warnings and instructions, then no real harm is done by stating: 'This product could cause injury'.

What is harmful is an admission of unreasonable and unnecessary risks.

How then can any safety improvement be proposed, failure reported, reservation expressed etc. without admitting that an unreasonable risk is meanwhile being taken?

Only by taking great care with the wording, approach and response. Tempting though it might seem, the policy of avoiding any documentation on the issue (or downright lying about it) could in the long term prove very costly: one day the truth might come out, and the producer's reputation will plummet. Better to admit knowledge of a *possible* risk and show what was being done about it than to be found guilty of a deliberate cover-up campaign.

Any documentation should therefore remain truthful, but expressed in a *positive and uncritical* manner.

● *DON'T criticise or blame others.*

It is a common ploy when something goes wrong to blame someone else. Engineering blames manufacturing for not achieving the standard specified, manufacturing blames purchasing for not getting the right quality from suppliers, and purchasing pass the buck to finance for imposing unreasonable cost limits.

Often these sorts of criticisms are not accurate, but over-generalisations to try to get oneself out of trouble: part of the 'cover your own backside' syndrome.

For the lawyer they are ideal evidence. Here is someone within the producer's organisation, presumably well-qualified, pointing out where the fault lies, virtually admitting liability. What could be better?

To avoid this, be positive when trying to point out that a problem might exist in some other department, instead of critical.

Not: 'The problem obviously lies with poor quality control within manufacturing. Will they please carry out an immediate review of their procedures.'

Rather: 'Will manufacturing please review their quality control procedures to establish whether improvements are necessary.'

Similarly:

● *DON'T criticise the product.*

Criticism is a common pastime, particularly among service engineers, parts suppliers and others involved in after-sales support. The customer seeking the repair or replacement part is all too often greeted with: 'Common fault this; they're all like it. Poor design.'

Or: 'The early models were plagued with defects. The new ones are a lot better.'

The harassed service receptionist may easily agree with the complaining customer that the product is a complete and utter disaster, rather than suffering a routine breakdown which can be remedied by a service. The fact that it breaks down does not mean it is defective: the comments might be treated as an admission that it is.

The introduction of a new model can lead staff to start denigrating the previous version, which suddenly seems hopelessly deficient. The reverse is sometimes the case: 'They don't make 'em as good as they used too'.

Either way, it could be taken as an admission that defects exist.

Observing these do's and don'ts will reduce the potential harm within the documents, but having raised a possible safety problem it is then vital that the producer can prove he is doing something about it.

This leads to the fourth and best solution:

Ensuring that if the document suggests that action can be taken to overcome the risk, then such action is taken and properly recorded, that is, the loop is closed

It may not be the writer's job to take the appropriate action personally, but he can take positive steps to ensure someone else does. This involves four more do's and don'ts:

● *DO request action.*

The purpose of communication is normally twofold:

(i)   to pass on information;

(ii)   to get action.

Too often this second purpose is forgotten in the routine of completing reports or investigations. The writer assumes that by simply providing the information the recipient will realise what action is required. That is not always so. The recipient may not grasp the significance: he may assume someone else is taking responsibility or that other matters have priority.

If something needs to be done the writer should request it.

Otherwise the loop he has opened may not be closed; the bomb will not be defused.

Suppose he has been asked to carry out a test on a plastic component to see at what point it fails and report the results. If the person to whom he is reporting is fully aware of the significance, then no request is necessary. But in many cases it is appropriate to suggest *something*. So, if the thing failed during the test he will give details of the circumstances in which it failed and then can add: 'Request product engineering carry out further investigation'.

That should be sufficient. He is merely a tester, not a designer, so he should not go on by speculating: 'The failure is due to an inherent structural weakness. The solution is to increase the thickness of the plastic', because he could be wrong.

If he genuinely believes that the plastic is too thin, then he can make the helpful suggestion: 'Please investigate possibility of increasing the thickness to prevent this failure'.

This may well be the solution, and his suggestion may save unnecessary investigation by engineering. He has passed on the same message, but not stated there is an actual defect or the need for a solution to it.

The potential for open loops is increased when a report has a long circulation list and does not indicate which people on that list are required to take action. The writer assumes that those responsible will realise. The individual recipient assumes someone else will take responsibility. The longer the list the greater this possibility, but often the writer thinks: 'The more people I tell, the more likely someone will do something'.

The report should clearly identify those on the circulation for whom it is 'information only' and those from whom action is required. On a long report this may need to be identified point by point.

● *DON'T request something that is not realistically obtainable.*

Prime candidates for this are engineers who recommend some potentially safer system *after* the product or process has been tested, approved and put into production. The existing product is not defective, but the recommendation seems to indicate that it is. That recommendation becomes an unexploded bomb.

Comments such as: 'What we would do in an ideal world is . . .', or 'If we had unlimited resources we would . . .' are to be avoided.

● *DO seek feedback.*

Having raised a safety issue, provided full information and requested action, the originator may think his job is done. The report is off his desk, now it is up to someone else. But he has set the bomb — he has opened the loop, and therefore has some responsibility for checking what action follows to defuse the bomb — to close the loop. If not satisfied he then has an opportunity press for further action.

It is not necessary to discover precisely what action has been taken, simply to know that the issue has been or is being resolved. To hope that action has resulted, or rely on some chance feedback through the grapevine, is dangerous. So the originator should include on his report a positive request for feedback, e.g., 'Please report back within 21 days on what action taken'.

Ideally the procedure itself provides for feedback, with documents designed accordingly. By providing the originator with feedback, he may feel less inclined to resort to the tactic of exaggeration to get a positive response.

● *DO retain copies of documents.*

Documents can be vital evidence for the producer in defending a case. If he is asked for proof that a test was carried out or a potential safety improvement assessed, a document is more conclusive than someone's memory. Cases have been lost through failure to retain documents, simply because the court can only make a judgment based on the evidence presented to it.

Particularly dangerous is the situation where *some* documentation can be found, but parts are missing. The presumption can then be made that, since the producer has a system for documenting these matters, anything not on it did not in fact happen.

With written communications the person raising the matter opens a loop, and ideally should have documented evidence of its closure. In practice that evidence may be elsewhere, usually with the person or department who took action. So while all those involved in that loop may not personally have possession of all the documentation they should retain their part of it. Too often documents are thrown away with the attitude: 'That problem has now been solved. There's no need to keep these bits of paper leading up to it.'

The responsible producer has a document retention procedure detailing what must be kept and in what form. In the absence of this the individual employee should play safe: if in doubt retain. When the filing cabinet is full get another cabinet or put on microfilm rather than throw out what could be vital evidence.

It is essential that the documents CLOSE THE LOOP.

SUMMARY

A victim's lawyers have extensive powers to extract information about the safety of the product. The producer cannot rely on hiding or tampering with any documentary evidence he has, or otherwise preventing the truth coming out. It is essential that staff realise the vulnerability of any documents to discovery, and the ways a lawyer might use the evidence in them.

Great care must be taken before committing safety-related matters to writing. Documents are the prime source of incriminating evidence, and can be self-damning.

Four solutions are possible, the first two of which are not recommended:

(a)   Not writing the matter down in the first place:

● Not always a practical solution, and may be ineffective because other evidence reveals the truth.

(b)   Destroying the documents before discovery:

● Difficulty of locating and destroying all copies.

● Severe embarrassment if found out.

(c)   Ensuring the contents are as harmless as possible:

● State facts.

● Give full information so that action can follow.

●   Do not speculate.

●   Do not give unqualified opinions.

●   Do not exaggerate.

●   Be conservative with remarks and conclusions.

●   Do not imply cost or resource constraints always take priority over safety.

●   Do not suggest unreasonable risks are being taken.

●   Do not criticise unduly.

   (d)   Ensure the documents show what action was taken.

●   Request action.

●   Seek feedback.

●   Retain copies.

The message in this chapter is not to tell lies, refuse to communicate problems or resort to double-speak by using words which do not convey the true facts. It is to communicate the truth, as clearly and fully as possible so that the message gets across and remedial action can occur, but not to create unnecessarily damaging evidence by dramatisation, exaggeration, criticism, unqualified opinions and guesswork.

NOTES

1   For details see the standard texts on the English legal system. In particular "Modern Developments in the Law of Civil Procedure", D.B. Casson & I.H. Dennis.

2   Supreme Court Act 1981, ss. 33 to 35; Rules of the Supreme Court, Order 24 et seq.

3   *The Compagnie Financiere et Commerciale du Pacifique* v *The Peruvian Guano Co.* (1882) 11 QBD 55.

4   *Shaw* v *Vauxhall Motors Ltd.* [1974] 1 WLR 1035 per Lord Denning MR.

5   *Grant* v *Southwestern & County Properties Ltd* [1975] Ch 185.

6   *Davies* v *Eli Lilly & Co.* [1987] 1 WLR 428, in which the court permitted a medical journalist familiar with computerised document systems of pharmaceutical companies to assist in the inspection of documents, which it was thought numbered about 1.2 million, relating to the drug Opren.

7   *Waugh* v *British Railways Board* [1980] AC 521.

8   *English & American Insurance Co. Ltd* v *Herbert Smith & Co.* (1987) 137 NLJ 148; *Goddard* v *Nationwide Building Society* [1987] QB 670.

9   *Anton Piller KG* v *Manufacturing Processes Ltd* [1976] Ch 55.

10   *Walker* v *Eli Lilly & Co.* (1986) 136 NLJ 608.

11   *Board* v *Thomas Hedley & Co. Ltd* [1951] 2 All ER 431, a dermatitis case in which the manufacturers of a washing powder were obliged to disclose letters of complaint and congratulation about the product from users both before and after the plaintiff suffered the injury. See also *Blakebrough* v *British Motor Corporation Ltd* (1969) 113 SJ 366.

12   *Waugh* v *British Railways Board* [1980] AC 521.

13   *Harrington* v *Polytechnic of North London* [1984] 1 WLR 1293.

14   *Warner-Lambert Co.* v *Glaxo Laboratories Ltd* [1975] RPC 354.

15   *Distillers Co. (Biochemicals) Ltd* v *Times Newspapers Ltd* [1975] QB 613.

16   In *Grimshaw* v *Ford Motor Co.* (1981) 174 Cal Rptr 348 the jury awarded $125 million punitive damages against Ford for a design defect in the placement and protection of the fuel tank on the Pinto model. Engineers' reports indicated that the protection could have been significantly improved at minimum cost.

8

General Management Strategy

This chapter examines the role of general management in laying down the policies and framework for managing the product liability risk. Chapter 9 will then examine the responsibilities of particular departments and functional areas.

Management strategy is based on recognising two key factors:

(a) The importance of marketing a safe product, and the potential cost of failing to do so.

(b) That failures will occur and plans must be made for mitigating their effect.

The needs of individual businesses will differ, but the following matters are common in any strategy.

COMMITMENT TO PRODUCT SAFETY

Little progress can be made by individuals within an organisation towards reducing the product liability exposure unless top management are committed to marketing safe products.

Safety is one aspect of the overall quality of a product. While most producers and suppliers realise the importance of quality in terms of sales and reputation, there is sometimes less thought given to the importance of safety in terms of legal liabilities.

Management should stress the organisation's strong commitment to product safety at every opportunity. Wherever 'quality' is mentioned it should be associated with 'product safety'. The very names of certain departments, committees and procedures could be changed to emphasise this. Similarly the notices, posters and training manuals exhorting employees to strive for quality should stress that this involves safety. It is essential that this commitment be communicated to employees at all levels and in all functions, because virtually everyone has the potential to raise or lower the risk by what they do, write or say.

Product safety policy statement

One way of publicising this commitment is by a policy statement, signed by the chief executive, prominently displayed and issued to employees, customers and other interested parties. This sets out briefly the importance attached to product safety and the intention of the organisation to prevent product liability claims arising. For example:

> It is the policy of this company to design, manufacture and supply safe and reliable products consistent with the best interests of the customer, user and general public. To this end management is committed to a continuing programme of research and investment. The implementation of applicable safety standards, both mandatory and as recommended by the appropriate standards authorities, is seen as a minimum requirement to be exceeded where possible.

> While always seeking to deliver products free from defects or safety hazards, the company will take steps to protect itself against legal liability by insurance and other measures. Each of us has a responsibility to the company as well as to our customers. Specific responsibilities will be a matter of management evaluation. Only in this way can we achieve the objectives of reducing the potential for accidents while maintaining continuity of business.

> Your support and cooperation are essential in achieving these objectives.

> [Signed] . . .
> Chairman and Chief Executive

TRAINING AND MOTIVATING STAFF

Staff attitude and awareness are vital factors in reducing the exposure. Most staff realise that safety is important, for commercial, legal and moral reasons. They may have a vague idea of the legal implications: victims of defective products have legal rights, the company could be sued or prosecuted, maybe they personally could be held liable.

But are they sufficiently aware:

- Of the costs of defending a product liability action, win or lose, both direct and indirect?

- That insurance may not cover the cost?

- Of the vulnerability of the things they write or record to discovery?

- How a lawyer will exploit the evidence, e.g., exaggerations, opinions and speculations used to emphasise a point will be treated as fact; doubts and reservations treated as admissions?

- That taking a risk on a product safety matter could be regarded as negligence and recklessness, leading to both civil and criminal actions and (at least in the United States) claims for punitive damages?

- How vital it is to retain documents for use as rebuttal evidence?

- Of the danger of 'open loops'?

- That the law is now much tougher?

Improving staff attitude and awareness means providing training, information, opportunities for discussion and constant reminders to *think of the implications*. Suggestion schemes, quality circles and the like are only part of the answer. Staff must be encouraged to think in terms of how their actions and words would appear in the context of a product liability claim being built up against them.

Such training can be given when staff first arrive, forming part of any induction course.[1] It should be a regular part of continuing training provision, including new information on the interpretation of the legislation, recent experiences of other companies, changes in the company's own procedures.

Guidelines can be issued on such things as report-writing, handling customer complaints, reporting faults: short, terse lists of the dos and the don'ts to remind staff of the pitfalls.

FORMING A PRODUCT SAFETY COMMITTEE

It may be useful to form a product safety committee, particularly in larger organisations where the various departments tend to operate independently and at some distance from each other. Its membership should include senior members from each of the major functional areas, chaired either by the chief executive or a very senior manager to reflect its importance. The company's lawyer should be present if possible. If not, then copies of minutes and matters arising from the meetings should be referred to him.

Its terms of reference might include:

● Creating and monitoring a product safety programme.

● Discussing product safety issues referred to it by individuals, departments or committees.

● Coordinating efforts between different departments and functions to improve product safety.

● Receiving reports on accidents, warranty claims, technological developments, legislative changes etc. and recommending appropriate action.

● Handling emergency situations, such as major product accidents, product sabotage, recalls, which cannot otherwise be dealt with by routine procedures. Having an established committee makes it possible to react quicker.

The committee should have such power and influence that its recommendations are invariably implemented. Failure to do so could be interpreted as negligence or recklessness, and have serious repercussions for the defence of any future legal action.

The discussions of the committee need to be very carefully minuted. Such minutes could be subject to discovery. They could be vital in proving that a safety matter was discussed and a proper decision reached. Conversely they could reveal that a problem was raised but not resolved. The temptation then might be not to include this in the minutes, but the evidence might come out in some other way (as discussed in chapter 7) and make it appear as a deliberate cover-up. A compromise is to keep minutes in brief summary form, e.g., 'Discussed warning labels for the new machine', without detailing the discussion. Where the minutes show that a recommendation was made, it is essential that somewhere in the company there is documented evidence of the action that followed — so as to close the loop. Future minutes should note this under matters arising.

PRODUCT SAFETY COORDINATOR

A member of the product safety committee should be designated 'product safety coordinator', 'product control manager' or some similar title. He must be recognised as a part of senior management with access to *all* functional areas and operating levels. He should have a basic understanding of product liability law, at least to the extent of knowing when the company needs to seek expert legal advice. He will need an appreciation of engineering, manufacturing and marketing disciplines, sufficient to liaise with staff in those functions. He must have the ability and seniority to bring together into the decision-making process both in-house and outside members of the products team.

RISK STRATEGY

The obvious solution to the product liability risk is not to produce defective products, but in the real world nothing is absolute. Mistakes happen, risks sometimes have to be taken, products could be made safer, people get hurt from apparently harmless products. A strategy therefore has to be devised to manage the risk.[2]

This involves four elements:

   (a)   identifying and quantifying the risk,

   (b)   reducing the risk,

   (c)   transferring the risk,

   (d)   retaining the risk.

Identifying and quantifying the risk

●   Gather reports and statistics on the number and type of accidents caused by that product or others like it.

●   Apply techniques of hazard analysis and risk assessment to identify and prioritise potential risks, e.g., failure modes and effects analysis.

●   Monitor fault reports, warranty claims, incidents reported by field personnel, dealers and users.

●   Keep abreast of developments in science and technology, legislation and the environment which may indicate risks not previously apparent.

If the risk is very small, then a decision to do nothing to reduce it may be reasonable. The product may not be considered 'defective', or even if it is the consequences may be so minor that the risk is worth taking given all the circumstances.

Reducing the risk

● Design, manufacture and market the product to meet all anticipated safety expectations, despite the adverse effects on cost.

● Adopt a policy of going beyond minimum legislative requirements, rather than scraping through.

● Comply with voluntary national and international standards and codes of practice, e.g., BS 5750 (see Appendix 1).

● Ensure that suppliers meet high quality standards to minimise the possibility of defects in their materials and components for which you could be liable. Insist that they comply with BS 5750 or its equivalent.

Transferring the risk

● Identify suppliers, importers, co-producers. Have records and systems to trace defective products back to the parties responsible, so that they can be joined in any legal action.

● Check that they have adequate resources and/or insurance to meet their liabilities.

● Incorporate contract terms which provide for recourse and fair apportionment of damages and costs. Ensure that one's own terms apply, i.e., win the 'battle of the forms'. If suppliers insist that their terms shall apply, then try negotiating for better terms.

● Take out insurance.

Insurance seems the safest solution, but there are problems, notably the cost of the premium and the extent of the cover provided. Some of the factors to be considered are outlined below.

In deciding how much cover is needed, the producer or supplier must predict all the possible expenses of a major product failure: not just the damage and injuries likely to be suffered, but consequential expenses such as recall, rectification, redesign, loss of sales. Where the product (or in the case of a component the product in which it is incorporated) is exported or likely to circulate in other countries he must consider the possible claims arising there. In the USA these could be enormous. In the EC the effect of derogations (e.g., no development risks defence in certain member States) and of the Brussels Convention (to facilitate forum shopping) should be considered (see chapter 3).

The ideal product liability insurance policy would indemnify the insured for all sums that he is required to pay by way of settlement of claims (whether via court action or negotiation), plus consequential losses and expenses. All this for a reasonable premium, of course!

In practice there will be significant limitations. Insurers frequently define three broad categories of insurable product risks as:

(a) 'Product liability': the cost of meeting claims by third parties for personal injury and property loss, plus their consequential losses, caused by defective products. Not usually the cost of damage to the product itself.

(b) 'Product guarantee': expenses incurred by the repair, replacement, treatment or other rectification of the defective product.

(c) 'Product recall': expenses incurred by recalling defective products.

Many producers who assume they are adequately insured may in fact only be covered for category (a), and when they do suffer a major product failure will incur enormous irrecoverable costs.

Within the categories there will be limitations and exclusions which need to be carefully considered, such as:

● A deductible or excess: the insured bears the first part of the loss, up to a specified figure or percentage. Is this too high? How will it be paid? It could prove crippling if there are numerous separate claims. For a slightly higher premium a lower deductible may be available.

● A ceiling on the cover. Expressed usually as a maximum per claim and an aggregate for the year. While the total might seem adequate, remember that liability under CPA 1987 is unlimited and cannot be excluded. Could a major disaster, or a series of smaller ones, take liability beyond the ceiling? A relatively small increase in the premium may significantly increase that ceiling.

● 'Design, formula exclusions' which exclude liability for errors in the design, formula, specification or plans of the product, i.e., design defects. Cover is thereby restricted to manufacturing defects. For an increased premium such exclusions can be deleted.

● Certain risks not covered, e.g., restricted to 'accidental' damage rather than any damage howsoever occuring (from tampering etc.); excluding any products fitted in aircraft; territorial limits which exclude or limit liability arising in certain countries.
Careful reading of the small print of the policy is vital to decide whether such exclusions need to be negotiated out.

● Certain consequential costs not covered, e.g., product recall insurance may cover the direct expenses of tracing, recovering and modifying defective products but not of checking other kindred products where no defect has been reported, nor of disposal costs if the product cannot be rectified. Only by giving proper thought to the foreseeable expenses can the producer decide whether the policy is adequate.

Product liability insurance is frequently part of a combined policy covering also employer's liability and public liability. Such a policy may not be adequate, and expert advice should be sought on suitable alternatives. This may mean finding a specialist: not all insurance brokers are sufficiently experienced to offer such advice.

The premium and terms depend on the insurer's assessment of the particular risk. Factors include the type of product, quantity sold, countries to which it is exported (especially USA), previous claims history, the general state of the insurance market for such products.

Some insurers make no detailed assessment, simply asking the client to complete a questionnaire and offering a standard policy at a standard premium. Increasingly they are looking more closely at the client's risk management and loss prevention techniques. They can provide positive advice on these matters.

In any insurance contract the doctrine 'uberrimae fidei' applies, i.e., 'utmost good faith'. This makes it a duty of the insured to disclose all material information which might affect the insurer's decision to accept or reject the risk and fix the premium. Failure to do so enables the insurer to avoid the contract, i.e., refuse to pay any claims arising. For example, if the insured previously exported 20% of his production and obtained cover on that basis, then any significant increase in his exports would be a material fact to be disclosed. It is therefore vital to inform the insurer of any changes to the product itself or its distribution.

Another factor to consider is whether the policy operates on a 'losses occurring' or a 'claims made' basis. The former provides indemnity for losses occurring during the policy period, so if an accident occurs during 1989 but the actual claim is not made until 1990, then the policy in operation in 1989 will pay the claim. 'Claims made' means that the policy operating when the claim is actually made will pay, i.e., the 1990 policy covers the loss.

'Losses occurring' has the advantage to the insured that if he cannot afford insurance in later years, or the terms deteriorate, he still has cover for previous years up to the policy limit. It has the disadvantage that if a major catastrophe happened during one year, then the limit for that year might be exceeded and cannot be spread over later years during which the claims come in. He will have to decide during the current year the limit he needs to purchase to cover claims coming in for several years ahead, with allowance for inflation.

'Claims made' means the insured only has to decide on the limit he needs to cover claims during the current policy period. He may be aware of the likely claims outstanding from defects that have already caused loss. He can also better assess the effects of inflation. The major disadvantage is that if a disaster occurs or a major claim is made just before renewal of the policy and it is clear that large claims will follow, then the insurer might either refuse to renew or set a very high premium.

The trend in recent years, certainly for more hazardous products, has been for 'claims made' policies. This has been primarily at the insistence of the insurance companies rather than their clients. On renewal, an insured may be faced with a 'claims made' policy replacing the previous 'losses occurring' policy. He should seek clarification and advice on the implications.

Retaining the risk:

Having decided that the risk cannot be further reduced or transferred, the producer has to plan how he can bear it. Three possibilities are:

(a) *Special funds:* setting aside sums each year to build up a reserve fund to meet product liability expenses not covered by insurance.

The advantage is that the reserve will absorb these expenses without upsetting other financial planning. The disadvantages are that money is tied up which could be put to more positive uses; the fund has to be capable of being readily converted into cash, so investment opportunities are limited; the sums put aside are not deductible from taxable profits like insurance premiums (though payments made from the fund would be tax-deductible expenses).

(b) *Self-insurance:* instead of paying huge premiums to an outside insurance company for limited cover, the producer sets up his own 'captive' insurance company as a subsidiary.

The attractions are numerous: only one insured party; no need to make a profit, but any profit stays within the group; any type of loss can be paid without exceptions or limitations; premiums enjoy tax benefits; no great overheads with premises or large numbers of staff. However, only larger companies will be in a position to do this, due to the minimum capital requirements laid down by legislation for forming an insurance company. There are strict rules on maintaining reserves, investment and disclosure of accounts. The insurance company will in practice reinsure to spread the risk, so there will not be total independence from the insurance market.

(c) *Using the device of separate corporate personality and limited liability:* structuring the company into a parent with a number of separate subsidiaries.

Each subsidiary handles a particular part of the business. So, company ABC Ltd wishes to develop a new product but is concerned at the product liability implications. It incorporates a wholly-owned subsidiary ABC (Special Products) Ltd, capitalised at a nominal amount, say £100, and vests in that subsidiary the patent rights, trade mark and manufacturing facilities to develop and market that product. The rest of the financing is provided by the parent, ABC Ltd, but does not form part of the capital base. If ABC (Special Products) Ltd then becomes liable for a huge claim it alone pays, up to the value of its own capital, assets and insurance. It goes into liquidation. ABC Ltd, as a separate legal entity, bears no liability beyond the value of its shareholding in the subsidiary, £100. (There are exceptions to this 'veil of incorporation', see below.)

When this example was raised in the House of Lords by Lord Williams of Elvel, the opposition spokesman, during the committee stage of the Consumer Protection Bill it was agreed by Lord Lucas of Chilworth, for the government, that the subsidiary would be treated as 'producer'. This would mean, as Lord Williams pointed out, that if damages were assessed at £1 million then the parent would simply put the subsidiary into liquidation, bear no further responsibility and leave the victim uncompensated, thereby rendering the whole purpose of the legislation ineffective. Lord Lucas agreed that this was legally possible, but doubted that it would arise in practice. He argued that the avoidance of potential liability was not likely to be a predominant factor in the structuring of companies; that if a group of companies were large enough to be able to sacrifice a subsidiary in this way, then it is more likely that it would be able to bear the loss or have secured adequate insurance in the first place; that it would be more concerned with maintaining the reputation of the whole group than avoiding its legal and moral responsibilities: if the parent is prepared to use this device, then who would be prepared to deal with that group in the future? He also referred to other statutes, such as the Insolvency Act 1986, under which the directors might face disqualification or other penalties.

On the last point it seems unlikely that a director would face proceedings unless the business had been carried on with intent to defraud creditors or his conduct makes him unfit to manage a company.[3]

Lord Lucas may be correct in his conclusion that business is not conducted with a view to avoiding liabilities but, as Lord Williams concluded, there are all sorts of ways of structuring companies, registering them in overseas tax havens, forming trusts, using licensees etc., which have this effect. The question of whether a parent believes its reputation would be harmed or its directors might risk disqualification is a quite different issue from making it legally liable.

The principle of separate legal personality has been long established in English law[4] and recognised by the courts as a perfectly legal device for the actual owners of a company to distance themselves from its liabilities. Only in exceptional circumstances will a court 'lift the veil' to place liability on the actual owners or controllers. The veil will not be lifted simply because one company (parent) is the majority shareholder of another (subsidiary). But if the parent exercises control to the extent that the subsidiary becomes purely its agent, then an exception may be made. In one such case[5] an individual shareholder had control over a number of companies. Lord Denning MR commented:

> He controlled their every movement. Each danced to his bidding. He pulled the strings. No one else got within reach of them. Transformed into legal language, they were his agents to do as he commanded. He was the principal behind them. I am of the opinion that the court should pull aside the corporate veil and treat these concerns as being his creatures — for whose doings he should be, and is, responsible.

American courts, applying the same general principles of corporate theory, have shown a slightly greater willingness to lift the veil. In a case arising from an aircraft crash in Nicaragua an allegation was made against Rolls-Royce, makers of the engines. These had been supplied by Rolls-Royce Inc., a Delaware corporation whose shares were entirely owned by Rolls-Royce of Canada Ltd, which in turn was wholly owned by Rolls-Royce Ltd of England. The court held that Rolls-Royce Inc. was sufficiently controlled by Rolls-Royce of England Ltd that it should not be treated as an independent body.[6]

So a subsidiary company needs to be given sufficient independence from its parent to maintain the façade of separate corporate existence. Any company proposing to establish a subsidiary with a view to distancing itself from future liabilities should take expert legal advice on how it should be structured and organised.

The device is not therefore quite as simple and attractive as first appears. It is legally permissible and will be of increasing significance in decisions on company structures. It is certainly something to beware of when checking the financial viability of suppliers and co-producers.

PLANNING FOR THE UNTHINKABLE

When the crisis of a major product failure occurs, it is too late to start planning how to minimise its effects. The procedures need to be already in existence. The attitude: 'We'll worry about that when it happens' can lead to unnecessary expense, loss of reputation and increased legal liability.

The reaction of the producer or supplier to the crisis may affect his legal liability in three ways:

(a)   Failure to have contingency plans for dealing with a foreseeable risk could be negligence.

(b)   The pressure of handling the crisis may lead individuals into speculating on causes, responsibilities and the extent of the problem. These could be treated as admissions that the product was defective or that there was negligence, which will be hard to deny later when the true facts are known.

(c)   If there is no effective way of warning others at risk, withdrawing stocks, recalling or otherwise preventing further exposure, then the number of potential claims will multiply out of control.

The crisis can result from some major disaster where people are killed and injured, such as a crash or explosion; from recently discovered side effects, such as with drugs or chemicals; from threats by tamperers of consumer products; or at a more mundane level from a minor incident, customer complaint or warranty claim highlighting an unforeseen problem.

At whatever level, advance planning can help mitigate the effects. Procedures should be prepared for such things as:

● getting emergency teams and equipment to victims at the scene of an accident; liaison with rescue and emergency services;

● immediate investigation of the causes and extent of the problem;

● handling enquiries and accusations of blame from the public, the press and particularly from victims' lawyers who will be looking for early admissions;

● warning other users who may be at risk;

● withdrawing stocks of similar products;

● recalling and rectifying affected products.

The planning process may require the assistance of outside consultants: few managers will have the experience or foresight to handle a major crisis.

The process generally involves four stages:

(a) An inventory of strengths and vulnerabilities: putting leading questions to managers and experienced staff from all functions to identify potential problem areas.

(b) Formulation of a response strategy, i.e., a manual of procedures for handling each type of crisis that can be foreseen.

(c) Testing the procedures by way of simulation exercises. The written procedure may not work in practice. By simulating a crisis any flaws can be identified and remedied. Such an exercise also fulfils a training function.

(d) Follow-up and review. The procedure must be regularly updated in response to developments both within the company and externally, e.g., new products and markets, the experience of other producers, new techniques of crisis management.

RECALL

A recall is a means of limiting claims. Under strict liability principles the fact that a producer has initiated a recall cannot prevent him being liable for any damage or injury meanwhile caused by the defective product. However, if a user receives a recall notification and ignores it, this may amount to contributory negligence, i.e., if he then suffers any loss, the damages payable will be reduced.

There is no compulsion to carry out a recall (see chapter 5), but failure to do so will increase the possibility of claims for damages. It will also have a very negative effect on the company's reputation and its future insurance premiums.

A recall plan should be devised, in advance, to cover the variety of scenarios that could occur. A committee, similar to the product safety committee, should be designated with effective power to coopt additional members as necessary into an action group to handle the particular recall. As soon as a recall is decided upon, then either the chairman of the committee or a senior manager should be appointed as overall coordinator.

Traceability is the key to the success of a recall. If it is possible to identify the batch or period during which the defect occurred, then the recall can be limited in extent. If there is no such means of identification, then the recall will be unnecessarily wide, more costly and probably less successful. Obviously traceability has to be built in: it cannot be created retrospectively. Consideration should be given to all practical ways of coding, batching, recording names of distributors and, ideally, the names of individual purchasers against code numbers. It may be feasible to enter the actual serial or batch number on sales invoices, delivery notes and other documents along with the purchaser's name. Greater use might be made of registration cards at point of sale. Component suppliers could suggest to end-product manufacturers that it is to their mutual advantage that the component serial number is included in records relating to the final product.

For the immediate purposes of a recall it is necessary to trace *downstream* from the point of production through end-product manufacturers (if a component), distributors and retailers to users. But traceability *upstream* is equally important. Can the precise point in the production process be identified as causing the defect? If so, corrective action can be taken to prevent recurrence. Can the materials or component parts be traced back to particular suppliers? If so, they can be joined in any court action; recourse can be sought for the expenses of the recall; they can be required to improve their quality control or be deleted from the list of suppliers.

Recall is an ideal subject for a simulation exercise. Assemble a group of managers, give them details of a hypothetical fault in the product and see how well it could be traced. Work out the likely costs and success of a recall campaign — that might well focus attention on the need for a better system!

SUMMARY

Effective management of the product liability risk demands a commitment to marketing safe products and a strategy to mitigate the effects of failures.

The commitment can be reflected in policy statements, training of staff, appointment of a product safety committee and a product safety coordinator, as well as by setting high safety standards in design, production and marketing.

Product risk management involves the four elements of risk identification, reduction, transfer and retention. When the risk cannot be further reduced or passed on to suppliers and co-producers, then insurance can provide a safety net. Any residual risk will have to be retained, but can be provided for by reserve funds or self-insurance.

The device of forming a subsidiary company to market a product and bear any subsequent liability has its attractions but may not always enable the parent company to distance itself: a court may 'lift the veil'; those dealing with the subsidiary may insist on guarantees by the parent; there are possible penalties for directors.

Planning must be on the basis of the worst possible scenario, with procedures in place to cope with the aftermath of a major product failure. If not, lawyers acting for defendants can exploit the weaknesses.

NOTES

1   There are now some excellent videos available, e.g., *When Products Harm,* obtainable from Product Liability International, Lloyd's of London Press, Sheepen Place, Colchester, Essex CO3 3LP. Telephone 0206 772022.

2   For an excellent review of such techniques see Howard Abbott, *Safer by Design,* (London: Design Council, 1987).

3   See Company Directors Disqualification Act 1986.

4   *Salomon* v *A. Salomon & Co. Ltd* [1897] AC 22.

5   *Wallersteiner* v *Moir* [1974] 1 WLR 991.

6   *Taca International Airlines SA* v *Rolls-Royce of England Ltd* (1965) 204 NE 2d 329 (New York); similarly *Brown* v *Volkswagen of America Inc.* (1983) 443 So 2d 880 (Alabama); *Continental Bankers Life Insurance Co. of the South* v *The Bank of Alamo* (1979) 578 SW 2D 625 (Tennessee). See D. Owles, 'What is a producer?', *Products Liability International,* April 1987.

9

Responsibilities of Particular Departments and Functions

Previous chapters have discussed the nature of product liability and the general tactics that can be adopted by producers and distributors to minimise the legal exposure. In this final chapter the aim is to highlight the implications for particular departments and functions by summarising the pitfalls and tactics which are specific to them. This will involve repeating many points made earlier, but in the form of checklists for ease of reference.

RESEARCH AND DEVELOPMENT, PRODUCT ENGINEERING, DESIGN

The pre-production or design phase of a product is crucial because it is here that the product's configuration and, therefore, much of its potential for harm, is determined. Those engaged in product design must therefore give high priority to the elimination or control of the hazards associated with the product. This may have to be to the detriment of ease of manufacture, styling, user convenience, price and other marketing factors.

Ideally, the decision-making process should take the following order of precedence:

(a) Recognise the existence of a potential hazard from research, testing and feedback.

(b) Eliminate or 'design out' that hazard.

(c)   Control or protect against occurrence of the hazard.

(d)   Provide effective warnings and instructions concerning any residual hazards.

The pitfalls

● Inadequate testing due to time, cost or resource constraints.

● Rejecting a safety-related proposal on cost or resource grounds alone.

● Not assessing a potential safety improvement.

● Failure to cater for predictable misuse of the product.

● Lack of documentation on design and test work, especially on reasons for rejecting a proposed safety feature, or deleting an existing feature.

● Failure to retain documentation for the period during which it might be essential in defending against design defect allegations. Potential liability under CPA 1987, Part I, extends for 10 years from the time of supply, not of design.

● Exaggerating the dangers of not having a particular safety feature.

● Speculation, without supporting evidence, on

  (i)   causes
  (ii)   consequences
  (iii) solutions

for an actual or potential design problem.

● Denigrating existing or earlier products. Extolling the safety virtues of the new design can imply that other or previous models are dangerous.

● Failure to inform other departments of design features, limitations and dangers (especially sales and marketing who might then misinform the customer).

● During production giving approval to requests for concessions or deviations from the specified design without fully testing for the possible effects.

The tactics

- Allocate sufficient time and resources to the design stage: the penalties for rushing into production could be enormous.

- Consider what safety features are known in the industry, and be extremely wary of omitting such features, especially if they appear on a competitor's equivalent model or other models within your own range.

- Use appropriate techniques, such as failure modes and effects analysis, to evaluate all potential risks of failure and their consequences, both from normal use and foreseeable misuse.

- Create and retain necessary documentation. Ensure there are no 'open loops'.

- Do not get over-enthusiastic about alternative designs, exaggerating their benefits as a means of trying to get them adopted. When making comparisons with competitors' designs, be objective: report the facts, avoiding opinions about how much better or worse the design might be.

- Do not speculate. Make predictions, where appropriate, based on evidence from testing, experience or other hard facts. Use statistical probabilities, not vague guesses.

- Consider the impact of new designs on existing or previous versions. Stress that the other versions are safe, or were considered safe when originally supplied: the new one has additional safety, reflects advances in technology or legislative requirements, is designed for specific purposes which necessitate the additional feature, not that the new one has been designed to overcome safety problems in the old.

- Ensure that other departments, suppliers, distributors, installers, repairers etc. are aware of the limitations of the design and react accordingly. Make the information intelligible to those who may not have so much design, engineering or scientific knowledge. Check any technical information issued by sales and marketing, service and other outward-facing functions for accuracy.

- During production any requests for concessions and deviations should be considered under the same procedures as for original design. In practice this may not be feasible, due to commercial pressures, e.g., production will stop unless the concession is granted. If full evaluation cannot be made immediately, ensure records are kept of serial numbers, batch codes or other identification so that those products can later be traced for remedial action.

Many requests for concessions arise because the original specification was unnecessarily strict. The design should foresee the likely problems during production and allow realistic tolerances and alternatives.

PURCHASING

The purchasing department is likely to be the main point of contact with suppliers. It is essential to get the correct relationship to ensure (a) that their product is not defective and (b) if it is, that they bear the appropriate share of liability.

The pitfalls

● Choosing a supplier without properly checking his quality and safety standards.

● Implying that cost is the dominant factor in choosing a supplier.

● Delaying purchase of new safety-related products on cost or convenience grounds.

● Not fully informing a supplier of the intended use of his product.

● If his product is a component to be incorporated into yours, not allowing him to test that component fully *in situ*.

● Not informing him of later modifications to your product which could affect the integrity of his component.

● Failure to retain correspondence with suppliers, especially on their knowledge/concurrence of the intended use.

● Failure to inform them of their liabilities under current legislation, and the implications, especially the need to retain records.

● Dealing with suppliers who have inadequate resources or insurance to cover potential liability.

- Allowing suppliers to impose onerous contractual terms, i.e., excluding or limiting their liability for defects.

- Allowing them concessions from the original specification without fully evaluating the possible effects.

- Inadequate records on 'anonymous' products to trace back to particular suppliers.

The tactics

- When choosing a supplier check his quality rating. Consider insisting that he complies with a recognised national standard, such as BS 5750.

- Do not let cost force a downgrading of safety below the design criteria. If several suppliers can meet that criteria, then choosing the cheapest among them does not imply his product is unsafe, even though the alternatives may be safer. Make it clear in any documentation that the choice was on this basis.

  Obviously price is an important factor, and is something that is taken into account in determining 'what persons generally are entitled to expect' in the definition of 'defective'. If the designer has specified something that purchasing find is excessively expensive, then he may have to consider changing the design. Purchasing can tell him of the available alternatives and any limitations these may have, but the final decision must be the designer's. If cost forces a downgrading below the level which one's own expert has stated is desirable, then it is hard to argue that persons generally have had their expectations met.

- Give a full and unambiguous specification. The supplier has a defence if his product complies with instructions given, so he can benefit from any inadequacies in those instructions.

- Conversely, fully inform the supplier of the intended usage and leave it to him to use his expertise in deciding what is suitable. By giving him some or all of the responsibility for the choice of design, he cannot then benefit from the defence that the defect is due to the design of the finished product rather than his component part. Get a written 'sign-off' that he understands and agrees to the usage.

- Inform suppliers that as 'producers' they are jointly and severally liable for damage caused by defects in their products, and that they cannot exclude such liability to victims whatever is stated in their terms and conditions of sale. They will be expected to bear their share of liability and should make financial plans accordingly.

- Check the financial strength and insurance cover of suppliers. If it is a subsidiary with inadequate resources, insist that the parent company provides guarantees or includes it in the group's insurance. Threaten that unless they take out adequate insurance to cover potential liability, you will not purchase their products.

Many producers are now writing to their suppliers on the following lines:

Dear Sirs,

The provisions of the Consumer Protection Act 1987 have now come into effect. You are reminded that as a producer of components which are incorporated into our products, we both face potential liability for defects in any of those components. We trust that no such situation will arise, and that you continue to ensure that your manufacturing and quality control systems are rigorous in respect of potentially dangerous defects. However, we must ensure that if any claim directed to us is the result of defective component parts, then liability can be fairly apportioned between ourselves and our suppliers.

We therefore require your written confirmation that you accept responsibility where any claim is proved as being caused by the failure of your product or service. In addition we request the following information on your product liability insurance cover:

1. The financial limit per claim.

2. The total annual amount of cover.

If we are not satisfied with the adequacy of this cover, then we will insist that you increase it to an agreed level if you are to remain one of our suppliers.

May we remind you that the contractual basis for the purchase of components and materials is that the supplier undertakes to maintain control of his production, and that it is his total responsibility to ensure compliance with agreed specifications.

Our terms and conditions of purchase have been amended to reflect these matters.

Yours faithfully

● Check with your company's lawyer the terms and conditions of purchase to ensure a right of recourse. Remember that while none of the 'producers' can exclude or limit their liability to victims, they can agree how much they indemnify each other for the damages and costs incurred. Special care should be taken when purchasing from non-EEC suppliers, because as an importer you will be treated as if producer and could incur full liability to the victim.
Provision should be made for recovering all costs, not just damages paid out to victims, e.g., recall expenses, legal costs.

● Ensure your terms apply, i.e., you win 'the battle of the forms'. If you are not powerful enough to impose your terms, then at least try to negotiate with the supplier for improved terms.

● Keep records of specifications given to suppliers; changes and concessions agreed later; any claims made by suppliers on the standard, suitability or performance of their product; their knowledge of and concurrence with the intended usage.

● Do not allow deviations or concessions from the specification without full engineering approval.

● Keep written records of each instance of non-conforming goods received.

● Ensure traceability by having systems for coding, marking, dating and storing their products. This may mean keeping copies of individual purchase orders.

MANUFACTURING, ASSEMBLY, INSTALLATION, REPAIR

No matter how good the design and the quality of bought-in materials, it is the ultimate responsibility of the manufacturing arm to ensure that each individual product meets the safety requirements. Proof of a manufacturing defect would not be too onerous for the victim because of the right of access by the discovery process to design documentation, which will reveal that the design specification has not been met.

The pitfalls

● Deviating from design specification without obtaining approval.

● Inadequate process instructions, allowing variations, inferior quality, unknown and untraceable defects to occur.

● Inadequate training, poor supervision, apathy of operators, allowing defects to occur.

● Taking risks to maintain production targets, cut costs, save time, reduce effort.

● Unreliable, unnecessarily difficult or time-consuming tools, equipment or procedures, tempting operators to use different, non-approved methods.

● Failure to maintain adequate records, especially details of any concessions, deviations, introduction dates for new methods or materials. These could be essential for traceability of defects for later rectification.

● Failure to quarantine rejects, superseded materials or items requiring further attention.

The tactics

● At the design and feasibility stage the ability of the manufacturing process to conform consistently with the design specification should be fully evaluated, using techniques such as process failure modes and effects analysis, statistical process controls, extensive dummy runs with all foreseeable variables. These evaluations should be documented and retained during the production life of the product, plus (at least for non-perishables) 10 years beyond.

● Operate a quality assurance system complying with relevant standards, such as BS 5750 (see Appendix 1), and any other control and audit systems such as statistical process control. The use of such systems should identify variations in the manufacturing process and enable corrections to be made before the process runs outside the control parameters.

● Make available comprehensive process instructions plus all relevant drawings. There should be a formal system for up-dating these, removing outdated ones, checking they are accessible to operators and providing replacement copies. Keep records of these instructions for 10 years from when they cease to be operative.

● Operate a planned maintenance programme for plant and equipment, ensuring regular servicing, calibration etc. so that consistent quality is achieved. Keep records of both the procedure used and the dates and details of each service.

- All production personnel should be fully trained in the method of work and the quality control systems relevant to their area. They should understand the need for these systems and the implications of failure to implement them properly.

- Having laid down the instructions and procedures for producing defect-free products, it is vital that these are adhered to. The training, supervision, awareness and general attitude must be such that operators do not take risks or cut corners on safety-related work. Suggestions from them on improving procedures, cutting time, cost or effort should be encouraged, but not allowed to be implemented until fully evaluated and approved.

QUALITY AND INSPECTION

Quality and inspection personnel, whether part of a separate department or integrated within other departments, obviously play a central role in preventing defective products reaching the market.

A quality control system, however good, cannot always prevent defects occurring. If defects get through then, under strict liability, the producer will be liable. Compliance with British Standards or any other codes for quality assurance does *not* automatically provide a defence under CPA 1987, Part I — all it can do is reduce defects or provide a means whereby defects can be detected. It may perhaps avoid claims for negligence or recklessness, and provide a defence to criminal charges.

The control of the producer's own processes is not the only concern. Suppliers, sub-contractors and other co-producers also need to be checked. The principle of joint and several liability makes one producer potentially fully liable for another's defects. Supplier quality assessment programmes, quality audits or equivalents are just as vital as in-house controls.

Beyond the legal considerations the two obvious benefits of good quality control will be:

(a) Better sales, particularly to other producers who could become liable for defective components. Many producers now insist that their suppliers comply with the appropriate quality standard.

(b) Better insurance. The availability, cost and extent of cover will depend on the insurance companies' assessment of the risk, and with the increased exposure created by CPA 1987 they are becoming more particular about their clients' quality control systems.

The pitfalls

● Not giving sufficient priority to quality control.

● Inadequate, outdated or unworkable quality or inspection procedures.

● Having set the appropriate quality or inspection procedure, failure to work to it consistently.

● Lack of control over suppliers and co-producers.

The tactics

● Quality must be continually stressed as the single most important factor in producing defect-free products and avoiding liability claims. A *quality system* should pervade throughout a company, covering design, purchasing, manufacturing, distribution, after-sale support, training and other functions. All personnel should understand the need for quality and contribute towards it in an integrated way. The personnel employed specifically on quality control should be enthusiastic and given sufficient authority to implement procedures. They should not be viewed as non-productive, interfering characters to be resented or ignored whenever possible.

● The quality procedures must reflect modern techniques. Previously the emphasis has been on *detection* — inspection *after* a manufacturing process to check for defects. Such inspection is usually on a sample basis, the results of which are used to conclude whether or not the rest of the batch is acceptable. Such conclusions rely on statistical probabilities, leaving the possibility of defects getting through. It only needs one defect to lead to a strict liability claim.

The modern approach is *prevention* — the process is set up *before* production to ensure that all items are produced within specified acceptable limits. Production is then monitored and kept under statistical control. As variables creep in and produce results towards the tolerance limits, then corrective action can be taken. With computer-controlled process equipment this correction can occur automatically, otherwise manual intervention is required. Defects should therefore be eliminated by controlling the process rather than the product that comes out of it.

Such statistical process control (SPC) systems have great advantages when defending liability claims. Evidence can be given that the process was highly unlikely to have produced the defect, because the batch from which the allegedly defective product came was produced within acceptable limits, i.e. the process could not have allowed it, rather than the detection system ought to have spotted it. SPC documentation should therefore be retained for 10 years.

● Insist that suppliers and co-producers implement appropriate standards. This should be done on initial selection of a supplier, and by regular audits to ensure continued compliance.

SALES AND MARKETING

The manner in which a product is marketed has a vital impact on product liability. The definitions of 'defective', 'merchantable quality' and 'reasonably fit for the particular purpose' are based on what it is reasonable for the consumer to expect in the circumstances. That expectation will be profoundly influenced by marketing. Sales personnel will be expected by the customer to have a superior knowledge of the design, performance and suitability of the product for particular purposes, including any safety hazards.

Inadequate warnings and instructions may be the result of marketing policy, e.g., not to alarm the consumer and put him off buying; putting styling and the brand image before the content and prominence of warnings; rushing to get the product into the market without proper consideration of necessary warnings.

Own-branding as a marketing policy now has the danger that the brander may be liable as if producer.

The pitfalls

● Raising consumer expectation beyond the capabilities of the product in sales and advertising literature, comments by sales personnel, packaging and instructions, e.g., superlatives such as 'fail-safe', 'completely reliable', 'childproof'.

● Misleading the consumer with inaccurate descriptions, information and claims about the performance of the product.

● Failure to point out dangers and limitations.

● Making unwise comparisons, e.g., that the old model is unsafe compared to the new one with its additional safety features, or the bottom of the range compared to the top.

● Recommending unsuitable applications, accessories, modifications.

● Stating that an optional safety feature is essential.

The tactics

● Give accurate information. If unsure, check. Do not guess. All claims about the product should be capable of being substantiated. Avoid claims which are unrealistic or unachievable by the average user. Advertising or demonstrations showing an expert performing stunts with the product can mislead the user into thinking it is safe for him to try to do the same.

● When giving any specification, description or statement about the product which cannot be 100% accurate, use tolerances, approximations or other qualifications. If the description or sample given to the customer may be different to what is later delivered, point this out and/or reserve the right to change the specification.

● Any limitations and dangers must be pointed out. Do not understate these. Consider potential misuse and abuse, especially when the product is supplied to a new customer or for a new purpose, and warn accordingly.

● Essential warnings and instructions must be given priority over styling, brand image and promotion. Do not obscure warnings by ineffectual wording, inconspicuous placement or making the product, brochure or packaging more attractive.

● Do not suggest that other models, past or present, are unsafe. A new or higher price model may have an additional safety feature: this must be marketed on the basis that the earlier version met the safety expectations at the time; that the cheaper version is safe, while the more expensive has an additional feature raising its safety above the standard normally expected.

● Optional safety features must be marketed without criticising the safety of the basic model. The limitations of the basic model and the benefits of the optional feature should be explained, particularly if it is known that the customer intends to use the product for a particular purpose for which the feature is necessary. But it must be emphasised that the basic model is safe for the purpose for which it is designed. Do not exaggerate the benefits of the option.

- If the product is own-branded, ensure that it is clear that someone else is the producer.

- Keep records of what brochures, handbooks, instructions, warnings, recommendations etc. were issued at the time of sale.

SERVICE AND AFTER-SALES SUPPORT

Those working in the service and after-sales support areas may feel that product liability has nothing to do with them. In fact it is here that a great deal of exposure can be created. First, because they influence the consumer expectation through advising on suitable usage, spares, accessories, servicing and repair. Secondly because they will be in contact with users of the product, including victims of defects, and so become aware of faults, deal with complaints, rectify defects, and make suggestions to colleagues in design, manufacturing and other functions on improving the product.

The pitfalls

- When offering spares, accessories etc. the same pitfalls and tactics apply as outlined for sales and marketing above.

- Becoming aware of actual and potential defects, but not communicating this knowledge back to those responsible for rectifying them.

- Not giving sufficient detail and accuracy in communications, thereby delaying any response.

- Exaggerating the problem as a way of making others take notice, thereby creating incriminating documentation.

- Understating the problem for fear of creating incriminating documentation, but thereby failing to convey the true nature of the problem and the need for corrective action.

- Recommending inappropriate solutions.

- Admitting liability.

●   Failure to 'close the loop', or retain records to prove that it was closed.

The tactics

●   Ensure the user gets the correct parts and information on installation and suitable usage. Warn of any hazards, limitations, need for future service etc. Stress the importance of using approved parts only. Warn of possible counterfeits.

●   When handling complaints, warranty claims, accident reports and any other incidents where it becomes apparent that there has been a product failure, get the facts and communicate them in full to those responsible for corrective action. Do not hide or understate the problem. Do not exaggerate or dramatise. Keep the report factual. Avoid speculation on causes, consequences or solutions. Do not admit liability or apportion blame.

●   Service personnel often feel they need to point out the possible causes and solutions of failures of which they become aware, that with their experience and being on the spot they can make a useful contribution towards corrective action. They must follow the dos and don'ts discussed in chapter 7.

●   When dealing with a complaining customer, do not imply that the product is defective. Sympathise, offer to help, promise to convey his complaint back to the designer or manufacturer, provide the necessary rectification, but do not admit liability. Avoid words like 'defect', 'neglect', 'common fault', 'blame' which can be interpreted as admissions. Use instead 'problem', 'breakdown', 'difficulty', 'failure', 'concern', which indicate the nature of the complaint but do not imply that it is due to defects in design, manufacture or marketing.

●   Complaints from customers, warranty data, feedback from service personnel, failure and accident reports should be summarised for review. Trends can be revealed and priority given to corrective action. Documentary evidence showing what action was taken must be retained — to close the loop.

FINANCE

Financial considerations loom large over every aspect of the design, manufacture and marketing of a product. Many products could be made safer if enough money were spent on them. The law does not require a producer to make limitless expenditure in the search for ultimate safety: it requires him to make the product safe in terms of meeting the public expectation and complying with specific regulations.

Achieving high quality and safety is a costly business. Most producers believe in the adage 'Quality pays' in terms of better reputation and sales, customer loyalty, lower reject rates, service and warranty costs etc. They should also realise that 'Safety pays' in terms of reducing the legal exposure and the tremendous costs that this can incur, both direct and indirect, e.g., high compensation figures, legal fees, the time and effort involved, increased insurance premiums, recalls, publicity.

It is the writer's experience that very few finance personnel are aware of the implications of product liability. Few attend training courses on the subject. They tend to think that product safety is the concern of those in design, engineering or manufacturing. Yet the greatest exposure is often created when someone in finance turns down a request for expenditure on a safety-related matter with the comment: 'It may improve safety, but it costs too much'.

The pitfalls

The single basic pitfall is that in seeking to control or reduce costs, the safety of the product is jeopardised, for example:

● Allowing cost to dominate a design decision to the extent that the product does not meet the consumer expectation.

● Inadequate expenditure on development, equipment, systems, training and any other resource.

● Turning down requests for expenditure on any safety-related matter without fully evaluating the risks involved.

● Imposing cost-cutting policies which reduce safety levels.

● Continuing to produce, use or supply outdated designs to avoid development costs, use up stocks, keep prices down.

The tactics

● In seeking to exercise financial control over the business, the finance department must balance cost against the potential risks. Any cost-cutting exercise or decision not to spend money on any matter affecting the safety of the product must be made with full awareness of the implications, legal and otherwise. Discussions must therefore be held with those in the company who have the appropriate awareness, e.g., from design, engineering, marketing, service and, often ignored but of vital importance, the legal department.

● Finance personnel should be educated on the legal implications and have access to legal advice.

● When the decision is taken not to spend, the full reasons must be documented. Cost should never appear as the ONLY reason. The design evaluations, test reports, comparisons, cost benefit analyses, perceived disadvantages of the proposed idea (apart from cost), market research reports and all other factors that were taken into consideration should be retained to later prove that a balanced view was taken.

LEGAL

The company's in-house legal department or the outside solicitors handling its legal affairs have an important role to play in reducing product liability exposure.

The pitfall is simply that lawyers are not sufficiently involved in the decision-making process. Often it never occurs to the engineers, scientists and managers to consult lawyers: safety is viewed as a technical matter which is no concern of the lawyers unless things go wrong, when they get called in to sort out the mess. To use a medical analogy, they are used as a casualty ward instead of being involved in preventative medicine.

The tactics

● Insist on greater involvement of lawyers in decisions affecting product safety: design, purchasing and marketing policies and documentation; production methods; markings, warnings and instructions; promotional materials; records; training.

● Offer to attend meetings, join committees (especially a product safety committee, for which a lawyer would be ideal chairman), give training talks.

- Set up systems for vetting internal and external communications, advertising, brochures, press releases etc. The clangers can then be filtered out before they cause a problem.
Inform colleagues that communications with lawyers can enjoy privilege in discovery.

- Be approachable. Create an atmosphere whereby those dealing with sensitive matters feel able to ask for legal advice.

- Review contractual terms with suppliers, purchasers, co-producers, licensees, dealers and others in the light of the new laws, e.g., your rights of recourse, their minimum insurance cover and financial backing (parent companies guaranteeing subsidiaries), quality standards. Existing terms may be inadequate, unenforceable and even illegal.

- Ensure that any incidents or claims on product safety are immediately investigated, evidence gathered before it goes cold, employees briefed on their responsibilities.

- Check that the company's record-retention system caters for future legal needs.

- Implement a rigid procedure for any offers for settlement of claims. Ensure that those in service and customer relations do not admit or imply liability when making such settlements. Provide a standard letter format for them to use and/or check the terms of each offer.

PERSONNEL AND TRAINING

Throughout this book emphasis has been given to the fact that much product liability exposure is created by a lack of awareness of staff of the legal implications of their actions. Staff need to be educated both on the nature of the legal situation and on the systems used by the company to manage the risk.

From the recruitment stage onwards, priority should be given to this. Job particulars, especially at senior level, should stress the company's commitment to producing safe and reliable products, and that the person appointed to the post will be expected to pursue this objective. The written product safety policy statement, if one exists, should be communicated at the earliest opportunity.

Training courses, for both new and established staff, should include sessions on product liability, report writing, the procedure for making suggestions on safety-related matters, the need to 'close the loop', the company's general approach to quality as well as the specific quality systems for the particular area where the employee operates.

Employees should not be made to feel paranoid about product liability. The approach should be positive, showing what pitfalls exist but that there are systems and tactics to control the risk.

Many employees are worried about their personal position if they do something which contributes to liability. They should be informed that the company, as producer, will be liable under CPA 1987 to victims of defective products, not individual employees. Similarly in contractual claims the company will be the seller or supplier, not the individual who negotiated the contract. If a claim is based on negligence, then the company, as employer, will be vicariously liable for the actions of individual employees. In criminal cases it will normally be the company that pays the fine — individuals are rarely prosecuted.

However, they should be reminded that in cases where an employee acts outside the scope of his terms of employment, is wilfully negligent or deliberately creates a hazard, e.g., by sabotage, then he may incur personal liability to the victim directly, or by the company seeking an indemnity from him, or taking disciplinary action which could include dismissal.

SUMMARY

Each department has a role to play in reducing the product liability exposure. Much unnecessary exposure is created by a lack of awareness among staff of the possible legal implications of their actions. By increasing this awareness through training, new procedures and policies, not only is the company likely to deliver a safer product but also be in a better position to defend itself against any claims that do arise.

Appendix 1

BS 5750: Summary of Main Factors Considered in Meeting the Standard

1 Quality system
(a)   Has the supplier established and documented a formal system of quality management?

2 Organisation

2.1 Personnel responsible for functions affecting quality
(a)   Has the supplier identified, and assigned responsibility for, the functions and activities directly affecting quality?
(b)   Are there any gaps?
(c)   Is there overlapping or conflict of responsibilities?
2.2 Management representative
(a)   Has a 'management representative' been appointed?
(b)   Has the representative the necessary authority, responsibility and ability to perform his functions effectively?
2.3 Purchaser's representative
(a)   When applicable is the purchaser's representative afforded reasonable access and facilities?

3 Review of the quality system
(a)   Does the supplier's management carry out periodic reviews?
(b)   Do these reviews make use of the findings of internal audits?
(c)   Does the supplier have a programme for auditing his quality system?
(d)   Are procedures for audit documented?

(e)   Are written audit procedures sufficiently comprehensive to provide objective evidence of the system's effectiveness?

(f)   Are audits planned and conducted systematically?

(g)   Is effective corrective action taken when revealed as necessary by the audit findings?

(h)   Are records of audits incorporated into the records of the effectiveness of the system as required by 4.6 of BS 5750 : Part 1 : 1979?

4   Planning

(a)   Has the supplier obtained all the information needed to execute the contract?

(b)   Has the supplier conducted a complete review of his contract to identify and provide for special or unusual contract requirements?

(c)   Has the supplier initiated quality planning prior to starting work?

(d)   Does the supplier's quality planning include identification of the need for developing new testing and inspection techniques?

(e)   Does quality planning provide for identifying material characteristics, or new or unique manufacturing processes, that affect end-product quality?

(f)   Are the plans and practical equipment compatible, for example, tool precision and inspection and measuring instruments?

5   Work instructions

(a)   Are documented instructions available for work operations where lack of instructions would adversely affect work performance?

(b)   Are such work instructions clear and complete?

(c)   Do they establish acceptable quality standards for the work operations covered?

(d)   Are they compatible with associated inspection and testing?

(e)   Is proper use made of the work instructions?

(f)   Are the work instructions sytematically reviewed?

6   Records

(a)   Are there records of essential quality assurance activities?

(b)   Are there effective means for assuring the currency, completeness and accuracy of records?

(c)   Do inspection records contain all essential data?

(d)   In instances of rejection, do records show resulting action?

(e)   Are records analysed and used for the purpose of management action?

(f)   Are there satisfactory arrangements for the storage and retrieval of records?

7   Corrective action

(a)   Does the system provide for prompt detection of inferior quality and for correction of its assignable causes?

(b)   Is adequate action taken to correct the causes of defects in material, facilities and functions, e.g., design, purchasing, testing?

(c)   Are analyses made to identify trends towards material non-conformance?

(d)   Is corrective action taken to arrest unfavourable trends before non-conformances occur?

(e)   Does corrective action extend to subcontractor material?

(f)   Is corrective action taken in response to user data?

(g)   Are data analysis and material examination conducted on scrap or rework to determine extent and causes of defects?

(h)   Is the effectiveness of corrective action reviewed and subsequently monitored?

8   Design control

(a)   Does the supplier's system provide for a planned programme of design and development?

(b)   Does this system cover the aspects of reliability, maintainability, safety, design review, value engineering, standardisation, interchangeability and documentation control?

(c)   Are design and development responsibilities clearly assigned?

(d)   Are design reviews carried out as part of the supplier's system of design control?

(e)   Does design review provide for assurance that the technical data created by design reflect contract requirements?

(f)   Is there an adequate system for controlling the issue and recall of this data?

(g)   Is there a procedure for proposing, approving and implementing design changes?

(h)   Is there appropriate control of design changes requiring approval by the purchaser?

(i)   Do the supplier's control procedures include his subcontractors and does the supplier monitor subcontractor changes requiring his approval?

(j)   Does the supplier's system provide adequate technical data for transition to the production phase?

9   Documentation and change control

(a)   Does the system provide for clear and precise stipulation of responsibilities in documentation issue and change control?

(b)   Are changes made in writing?

(c)   Is the system of recording changes satisfactory?

(d)   Are obsolete documents promptly removed from all points of issue or use?

(e)   Are changes relating to subcontracted material approved by the supplier or, under special arrangements, by the subcontractor?

(f)   Are the consequences of changes notified by subcontractors evaluated by the supplier?

(g)   Are the consequences of change on interchangeability and spare parts made known to the purchaser?

10   Control of inspection, measuring and test equipment

(a)   Does the supplier have a documented measurement and calibration system and does it meet the requirements of BS 5781 : Part 1?

(b)   Are necessary gauges, testing and measuring equipment available and used?

Note. For further typical questions reference should be made to appendix A of BS 5781 : Part 2 : 1981.

11   Control of purchased material and services

11.1   Purchasing

(a)   Does the system assure that material and services supplied by subcontractors meet contract requirements?

(b)   Does the system provide for the selection of subcontractors on the basis of their quality capability?

(c)   Does the supplier review his subcontractors' performance at intervals consistent with the complexity and quality of the product?

(d)   Do supplier records provide evidence that the supplier's controls, and those of his subcontractors are adequate to assure the quality of purchased material and services?

11.2   Purchasing data

(a)   Do the supplier's purchasing documents clearly describe requirements?

(b)   Are requirements for any necessary tests and inspection of raw materials specified in purchasing documents?

11.3 Receiving inspection

(a) Does the supplier inspect incoming material to the extent necessary upon receipt?

(b) Does the supplier adjust the extent of receiving inspection on the basis of objective data?

(c) Does the supplier assure that material conforms to the applicable physical, chemical and other technical requirements using laboratory analyses as necessary?

(d) Is tested approved material identified and carefully segregated from that not tested or approved?

(e) Does the supplier have effective controls for preventing the use of non-conforming incoming material?

(f) Are there adequate procedures for providing subcontractors with appropriate data regarding unsatisfactory quality?

(g) Has the supplier adequate controls for assuring correction of sub-contracted non-conforming material?

(h) Does the supplier's system provide for the immediate recall and replacement of material released for production prior to completion of receiving inspection and subsequently found to be non-conforming?

11.4 Verification of purchased material

(a) Do subcontracters afford the puchaser's representative the right to verify conformance at source when required by the contract?

(b) Are copies of documents necessary for such verification made available to the purchaser's representative in good time?

12 Manufacturing control

12.1 General

(a) Are all production processes accomplished under controlled conditions?

(b) Does control include necessary documented work instructions, adequate production equipment and appropriate working environments?

(c) Do necessary work instructions provide criteria for determining whether production, processing and fabrication work are acceptable or unacceptable.

(d) Does the quality system provide for monitoring both the issue of necessary work instructions and compliance with them?

(e) Are physical examinations, measurements or tests of materials provided for each work operation where appropriate?

(f) When direct inspection is not practicable, does the system provide for indirect control by monitoring of processes?

(g) Are both physical inspection and process monitoring used when either alone would be inadequate, or when required by the contract?

(h)   Are inspection and process monitoring accomplished systematically and are records kept?

(i)   Are unsuitable inspection or monitoring methods corrected promptly?

(j)   Is conformance to documented inspection methods complete and continuous and are corrective measures taken when non-compliance occurs?

(k)   Are acceptance and rejection criteria provided for all inspections and monitoring actions?

(l)   Are accepted and rejected material properly identified?

(m)   Does the quality system assure provision of the proper processing equipment as well as the necessary degree of certification, inspection, authorisation and monitoring for specified and complex processes?

(n)   Do established standards of workmanship and acceptance and rejection criteria provide an objective basis for decisions on acceptibility?

(o)   Can work be released without the agreement of the authority responsible?

12.2   Control of special processes

(a)   Do any of the supplier's manufacturing processes fall into the category of special processes?

(b)   Does the quality system ensure that appropriate and detailed work, inspection and test instructions are provided and used for any highly specialised or complex processes?

(c)   Is equipment used in special processes suitable?

(d)   Are personnel performing work on special processes adequately trained and qualified?

13   Purchaser supplied material

(a)   Does the supplier examine 'supplied material' upon receipt for damage, quantity, completeness and type?

(b)   Are there precautions and inspections during storage against damage and deterioration and to check on storage life limitations?

(c)   Is all 'supplied material' properly identified and protected from unauthorised use or improper disposal?

(d)   Have procedures been established for notification to the purchaser of any loss, damage, malfunction or deterioration of 'supplied material'?

14   Completed item inspection and test

(a)   Are completed items given a final inspection and test to establish overall quality?

(b)   Does the final testing meet the requirements of the relevant specification?

(c)   Are inspection and test problems or deficiencies promptly reported to the appropriate authority?

(d)   Is there reinspection and retest of all items that are reworked, repaired or modified after initial and product testing?

15   Sampling procedures

(a)   Are recognised standards on sampling being utilised or are supplier-designed sampling plans available for review by the purchaser's representative?

(b)   Do supplier-developed sampling plans provide valid confidence and quality levels?

(c)   Does the supplier enforce all of the conditions required for the application of the sampling plans used?

(d)   Are proper records maintained of sampling procedures and results?

(e)   Is there a clear indication of characteristics to which sampling is applied?

16   Control of non-conforming material

(a)   Does the supplier have an effective system for controlling non-conforming material.

(b)   Does the supplier properly identify, segregate and dispose of non-conforming material?

(c)   Are the procedures for repair and rework of non-conforming material documented and acceptable?

(d)   Are relevant scrap and rework data maintained and available for review?

(e)   Do repair and rework activities comply with documented procedures?

(f)   Are holding areas adequate for the segregation and storage of non-conforming material?

(g)   Has the supplier nominated personnel with authority to be responsible for review and designation of non-conforming material?

17   Indication of inspection status

(a)   Does the supplier employ an effective system for indicating the inspection status of material?

(b)   Is the inspection status of material readily apparent?

(c)   Is batch or lot identity maintained throughout the manufacturing process where necessary?

18   Protection and preservation of product quality

(a)   Does the system provide for the identification, as necessary, of the material from the time of receipt until the supplier's responsibility ceases?

(b)   Are adequate work and inspection instructions prepared and implemented for the handling, storage and delivery of material?

(c)   Are handling, storage and delivery procedures and methods monitored as part of the quality system review?

18.1   Material handling

(a)   Has the supplier instructions or procedures, where necessary, to control handling and transport operation?

(b)   Are special crates, boxes, containers, trucks or other transportation vehicles provided for handling material?

(c)   Are handling devices periodically inspected for cleanliness and suitability for use?

(d)   Is material suitably protected when passing through or held in areas that may contain harmful contaminants?

18.2   Storage

(a)   Are there procedures and regular schedules for the inspection of products in storage and are these procedures adequate to prevent deterioration or damage?

(b)   Is there a procedure to assure that items that can corrode or otherwise deteriorate during manufacture or interim storage are properly cleaned and preserved?

(c)   Are all required critical environments maintained during storage?

18.3   Delivery

(a)   Is all material to be stored or shipped properly identified and labelled?

(b)   Are all shipments prepared and transported in conformance to specified requirements and applicable carrier regulations?

19   Training

(a)   Are arrangements for personnel training satisfactory?

(b)   Are training records maintained?

Index